# HETEROPOLIS

CHARLES JENCKS

# HETEROPOLIS

### LOS ANGELES · THE RIOTS AND THE
### STRANGE BEAUTY OF HETERO-ARCHITECTURE

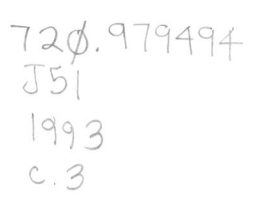 ACADEMY EDITIONS · ERNST & SOHN

# ACKNOWLEDGEMENTS

Editorial Offices
42 Leinster Gardens, London W2 3AN

Acknowledgements
Most helpful aid in tracking down the variety of plant life was given by Julia Russell, Nancy Power and Steven Sidawi of the Valley Research Corporation of L.A. I would like to thank Tulasi Srinivas and Robert Lerner for their help in preparing the maps and diagrams and for their many conversations on Los Angeles and its architecture. Maggie Keswick and Charlene Spretnak ironed out the wrinkled prose and strengthened the argument. To them and the architects – Frank Gehry, Eric Owen Moss, Thom Mayne, and Frank Israel – I owe special gratitude for making this book an enjoyable project to research and write. Allen Scott provided some helpful editorial suggestions for the second and third chapters which will appear in an anthology (edited by Allen Scott, Edward Soja and Richard Weinstein) University of California Press, Los Angeles, 1994. I would also like to thank the staff at Academy Editions, Lotta Elkiær, Nanet Mathiasen, Winnie Nielsen, and Meret Gabra for their help with the presentation of the maps and other material.

Photographic Credits
All photographs by Charles Jencks unless otherwise stated.
*Cover:* Frank Gehry with Claes Oldenburg and Coosje van Bruggen, *Chiat/Day/Mojo* Building, Venice, Los Angeles, 1991.
*page 2:* The hetero-architecture of the 1880s was carted off as the mono-architecture of the 1960s replaced it – here in the downtown residential area of Bunker Hill, the Music Center, background, heart of the cultural acropolis, will soon be challenged by Frank Gehry's Disney Hall. (Environmental Communications)

First published in Great Britain in 1993 by
ACADEMY EDITIONS
An imprint of the Academy Group Ltd

ACADEMY GROUP LTD
42 Leinster Gardens, London W2 3AN
ERNST & SOHN KG
Hohenzollerndamm 170, 1000 Berlin 31
Members of the VCH Publishing Group

ISBN 1 85490 186 9 HB
ISBN 1 85490 206 7 PB

Distributed to the trade in the United States of America by
ST MARTIN'S PRESS
175 Fifth Avenue, New York, NY 10010

Printed and bound in Singapore

# CONTENTS

# LOS ANGELES
# FUTURE OF THE HETEROPOLIS?

Los Angeles, like all cities, is unique, but in one way it may typify the world city of the future: there are only minorities. No single ethnic group, nor way of life, nor industrial sector dominates the scene. Pluralism has gone further here than in any other city in the world and for this reason it may well characterize the global megalopolis of the future. Mass migration threatens many cities in Europe, but in Los Angeles, with an influx of nearly a million foreigners in the last decade, it is a fact. The strains are obvious: homelessness, a variety of languages (more than eighty are spoken in the public schools), multi-ethnic tensions including riots, and a high rate of homicide.

Such depressing facts are well known to the outside world, but much less familiar is the urban and architectural response, both of which have been creative and positive. Spread out in a series of villages, high-rise centers and 'edge cities', the overall pattern resembles a map of Europe on a small scale. It is as if each distinct area such as the Hispanic Barrio or Beverly Hills were a tiny country with its separate language, set of customs and style. Yet there are no border crossings and in some of these tiny 'nations' many different populations mix together. The 'L.A. Nation' as a whole thus has a more dispersed ethnic mixture than many entire European countries, and it is this relatively fine-grained heterogeneity which I have tried to uncover and elucidate in a series of maps. They reveal more than an ethnicity that is diverse: they reveal some 'identity areas' which are highly defined and other fluid districts where variety is the rule. Difference and heterogeneity exist at many levels and this pluralism is itself a major reason why people continue to be drawn to Los Angeles.

It has also led to a new architectural approach and style: hetero-architecture. This strange sounding genre may represent variety as a sequence of opposed historical types, as Disneyland has done on a populist level, or the architect Jon Jerde has done on a commercial plane; or it may be an eclectic mixture of styles as in Charles Moore's work; or a set of different metaphors and contrasting materials as in Frank Gehry's. This last approach has become the shared method of

*OPPOSITE: (1) The beach scene, the Pacific Rim, the plains and the mountains – climate and opportunity, the reasons Los Angeles has grown as fast as any heteropolis this century. (Environmental Communications)*

the L.A. School of architects and it is most evident in the transformations of existing warehouses for new purposes.

The best of these are for the work-place, convivial bazaars where anything may happen, where many urban types coalesce: home, office, church, street, gallery and pub. Urbane and pluralist in the best sense, they bring together different voices and opposite styles; they are particularly suited to the small fast-changing and networked companies that occupy them for brief moments. The informality, improvisation and expressive abstraction are suitably heterogeneous and suggestive for a culture that neither wants to identify itself with a past situation, nor cut itself off from history. Ambiguous, sensuous and playful, these tiny urban villages turn inwards, defensive responses to a hostile, polluted environment.

Los Angeles, following New York, Chicago and San Francisco down the road of minoritization, faces the dilemma of multiculturalism at its most acute. Nowhere are the issues dividing America more pronounced: the imperative of the nation as a whole culture set against the desire for subcultures to flourish. *E pluribus unum* (out of many, one) is a formulation no longer adequate to that duality which many want: a dialogue between the one and the many, the center and the peripheries, with both sides equally acknowledged and allowed to talk. Hetero-architecture, which looks two ways at once, is beginning to achieve this, one answer among several for a democratic architecture of the future.

The major problem facing us today is obviously the destruction of the ecosphere and the mass-extinction of species, but a close second, and not unconnected, issue is the mass-migration of different ethnic groups into cities. A conservative estimate puts the figure at twenty million people on the move, those who are fleeing persecution and those looking for a better life. For the most part, they are heading towards global cities like Los Angeles. In this book I have used the concepts of a heteropolis and hetero-architecture to think about this phenomenon and the problems which are often debated under the rubric of multiculturalism. Architecture and urbanism do not reach the deep political issues, but they can cast a new light on the multicultural debate, which now dominates discussion in the United States and is beginning to preoccupy Europe. Hetero-architecture, as I see it, opens a third position in this discourse: to adopt current categories, it is situated on the edge of the battle between the fundamentalists and deconstructivists. It suggests a way of using otherness, hybridization and informality as creative responses to what is now an impasse: the conflict of dominant cultures with their subordinate minorities. Obviously it does not hold answers to the larger political questions, but it does suggest methods for confronting oppositions by creative displacement and creative eclecticism. It shows a way beyond entrenched positions. The love of difference – heterophilia – can lead to strange but beautiful inventions which diffuse strife by eliciting an enjoyment of and wonder at the Other.

## *MODERN* AND *POST-MODERN*

As the reader will find, I am, like many of the architects discussed here and many post-modern philosophers who will not be mentioned except in passing, a believer in pluralism, variety and difference as positive ends in themselves. Several different kinds of architecture will be illustrated in this text and, following post-modern poetics, I will switch voices suddenly depending on which tone is more suitable for a particular context. The wonderful yet horrible ersatz, for which Los Angeles is so celebrated and hated, deserves ironic detachment; historical and architectural events require narrative; the L.A. riots ask for a reportorial and political tone, while the overall scene can be surveyed from an aesthetic and philosophical viewpoint, especially when the complex question of multiculturalism is broached. Heterogeneity of architecture, and voice, is a goal to be nurtured.

However, the type of post-modernism I support, contrary to the deconstructive version, also embraces shared and 'universal' values, as well as their antithesis. One can express this antipodal morality in many ways; I have continued here and elsewhere to use the phrase 'double-coding' to indicate the opposition. The dual obligation towards the individual and group, part and whole, subculture and society has become a defining goal of post-modernists. One can find it expressed in countless ways across many fields from Arthur Koestler's concept of the holon (the fact that everything in nature is both a whole over a smaller part, and part of a larger whole), to Niels Bohr's principle of complementarity in physics, to Linda Hutcheon's notion of double-encoding in post-modern literature (the voice that speaks in and against the dominant). This is not the place to expound this philosophy, but it relates to a very important shift which I will discuss in the concluding chapter, the widespread movement underway today from Modern to Post-Modern Liberalism.

Modern Liberalism, which reached an early formulation in the American and French revolutions, represented a real advance on previous philosophies of government because of its insistence on universal rights, equality before the law and the dignity of the individual. These principles, now taken for granted even if they are not always put into effect, constitute what is called 'the politics of universalism'. While undoubtedly positive in themselves, they have led to some outstanding problems, above all the atomization of society into individuals and the suppression of minority cultures by the dominant, or 'universal', culture: in the United States this has invariably been WASP (White Anglo-Saxon Protestant). Hence Modern Liberalism has been challenged by 'the politics of difference' or what is more generally called multiculturalism.

Today marginalized groups and subcultures have, in effect, turned themselves into legal individuals; that is they ask to be accorded the same dignity and protection under the law that have been reserved for individuals under Modern Liberalism. They demand that their subculture be regarded with respect equal to that of the dominant group because they know from experience what sociologists and psychologists have been able to show: that self-worth and personal identity are fully realized only when one's culture is recognized and respected. The 'politics of difference' and the 'politics of universalism' are both valid, but they are based on contradictory axioms which make for continual conflict.

Many voices today are contributing to the evolution of a way beyond this impasse, a third position which would preserve the best aspects of the other two. For instance, Charles Taylor, a professor of philosophy and political science in Montreal, has shifted the divisive 'politics of difference' towards a more positive 'politics of recognition' while keeping the essential values of both the Modern Liberals and the multiculturalists.[1] His idea for a third way is a revised liberalism in which the state can support subcultures and engage in positive discrimination as long as the basic rights of others are protected. This Post-Modern Liberalism, to give it a name, presupposes a functioning Modern Liberalism as a prerequisite. The logic is straightforward: to be fair and effective the state cannot support particular subcultures unless, first, there is an abstract set of rights, equalities before the law, protection of other minorities and so on. In like manner the Los Angeles architecture of difference celebrated in this book depends on prior communal realities: a functioning economy and infrastructure and a sustainable ecology to name just three 'universals'.

Paradoxically, and paradox is often the message of post-modernism, Los Angeles has reached the stage where it cannot develop further, or perhaps even survive, unless it deepens a commitment to these contradictory liberalisms at the same time. As I argue in conclusion, it must rediscover the bounty of nature which has drawn people here for two centuries, and then uncover and start to love the variety of the peoples themselves. Heterophiliate or die! Such a bizarre notion only recently occurred to me after reflecting on a striking Los Angeles experience from twenty years ago, one whose deeper meaning has only become apparent in hindsight. This delayed vision – a Saul to Paul conversion on the road to downtown L.A. – was made with the aid of a book and a measure of reflection.

### HIDDEN VIRTUES OF LOS ANGELES

I was close to the official heart of the city, Bunker Hill, City Hall, the towers of commerce, but in one of those characteristic low-density residential areas with lots of Hockneyesque palms and variegated planting, waiting for a friend in her open-topped, third-hand Porsche (that is, in yet another type of L.A. nature) when suddenly I heard a dull thud right behind me. I looked around to find in the back seat a ripe avocado, an uninvited gift from the Southern California cornucopia. No question nature treats you well here; I saw why the architects of the 1880s (whose work was even then being dismantled on Bunker Hill to make way for the modernist leviathans) represented oranges, grapes and the many fruits that multiply here as long as the water is supplied. Although much had been made of the Los Angeles freeways, parking lots and endless asphalt by my teacher Reyner Banham, whose book *Los Angeles, The Architecture of the Four Ecologies* had just appeared, what struck me was not the tarmac but the endless greenery. The city was the opposite of New York, Chicago, Paris or any megalopolis I knew well because a network of living tissue seemed to run everywhere, connecting the villages and urban centers.

It was not until recently, when writing this book and after I accidentally came across an essay by the nature writer William Jordan, that I understood the significance of that dull thud. Los Angeles is not only a *ne plus ultra* of human pluralism but, thanks to the avocado and other gifts from the sky, it is the quintessential city of animal pluralism. This is the insight of William Jordan in his essay

'New Eden, City of Beasts' published in a wry collection of nature-observations *Divorce Among the Gulls*, 1991. Here we find the argument that the 'Big Avocado', L.A.'s self-aggrandizing answer to New York's 'Big Apple', provides sustenance for more animal diversity than any other comparable city. Rats, skunks, opossums and other unfriendly-to-man creatures live off this giant berry – rich in protein, fat and vitamins – but so too do coyotes, racoons, foxes, squirrels and those whom anthropomorphs tend to like (or like looking at). These and countless other species form a kind of counter L.A., a hidden order of citizens who come out at night and run along the garden fences, or overhead cables, or beside the roadside bushes, their equivalents to the freeway. It is not a safe environment, and many of them are unnecessarily killed crossing roads, or by a combination of pollution and variable food-source. But many of these uninvited guests prosper by keeping their wits about them, by staying out of sight and by marking their territory.

Of course they live off more than the avocado: fruits, nuts and berries from trees and vegetables stolen from gardens, and the highly nutritious and well-distributed garbage system create a mixed diet. Because there are so many front and back gardens stocked with ornamental shrubs that have edible parts, there is usually enough food to get by; as long as one is fairly small (no larger than a coyote) and has the right night-time habits plus a suitable disposition. Temperament, the ability to shut up and avoid too much human-based stress, Jordan argues, is the key virtue for survival. Animal pluralism, it turns out, has at least this parallel with the human variety.

*Homo sapiens*, it comes as no surprise to find out, is not particularly welcoming to his opportunistic cousins. In a typical year the L.A. County Department of Animal Control gets three thousand six hundred 'alerts', that is ten calls per day, to eradicate 'vermin', or 'pests': the stolid opossum like a large rat; the coyote that is often mistaken for a stray dog, sometimes at the expense of a bitten hand. A kind of Darwinian and Pentagonian struggle for existence is always going on; yet William Jordan's 'New Eden' manages to flourish.

I have no idea whether there is greater ecological diversity and more animal life today than in the eighteenth century when Los Angeles was mostly desert: it seems possible. Certainly more species run through its back alleys than in New York, or other American conurbations. They came, like the human population, from all corners of the globe: the roof rat from Europe and Asia, the pigeon from North

Africa, the parrot from South America and Australia, the opossum from the South and from eastern Texas. The coyote, two skunk species and the alligator lizard, among the major inhabitants, are native Californians. If one could draw an 'ethnic-animal map', showing the cultural background, land of origin and lifestyle of each species, perhaps it would be as varied as those for the human population.

This hidden diversity makes one reconsider certain attitudes towards political and cultural pluralism. It appears that animals, as much as humans, are opportunistic in their invasion of Southern California. Given the beneficent environment and the laid-back attempt to control them – the equivalent of malign neglect and *laissez-faire* applied to the population as a whole – they can sometimes flourish, or at least make their peace with the system. A price is paid for living in the cracks of human society, in the restricted niche of the gutter or attic or parking lot; in addition there are the senseless, accidental killings on the freeway. But one can imagine, if this hidden animal life ever becomes generally appreciated, that a positive relationship could be forged and the gift of animal profusion seen as essential to the city as is the climate and ocean. It would take a shift in attitude as great as that needed to appreciate the virtues of cultural pluralism. A new sensitivity to difference, both human and animal, would have to be developed along with a greater under-standing of the ecology on which they equally depend; that is a deeper sensitivity to actual Los Angeles reality and its unbelievable gifts: the avocado from the sky as well as the appreciated microclimates. The problem with natural beneficence is that it is often taken for granted and not loved until lost.

Obviously new rules of mutual respect and self-imposed restraints will have to be instituted if the opportunistic growth of the human and animal worlds are not to become self-defeating. Ever since Ridley Scott's film *Blade Runner*, 1982, predictions of a future Los Angeles dystopia have grown in number and credibility. The typical dark scenario of writers such as Mike Davis now predictably features corroding high-tech, no-go ganglands, runaway pollution, freeway shootings, child molestation, super-congestion, ethnic warfare and everyday violence. Indeed crime and homicide have risen yearly, even in 1992, in spite of a gangland truce and expressions of goodwill following the riots. Some commentators have predicted that Los Angeles could become a Beirut, yet another prosperous seaside paradise with a great future behind it.

The growing, changing megalopolis has analogies with other natural entities including the human body and mind. Its development follows certain broad stages towards more differentiation and reintegration, a somewhat linear course punctuated with moments of sudden economic and social crises followed by restructuring. What were primary considerations and attractions in Los Angeles (the promise of growth, unbelievable profits, open space, the gift of climate, freedom from the usual restraints of an historic city and all the things symbolized by the 'land of opportunity') become secondary or tertiary qualities to be reinvented or preserved; while the *results* of these attractions now come to the fore as primary: the pluralism of flora and fauna and featherless bipeds. To use an analogy from the science of chaos, the attractor of growth has suddenly jumped from economic individualism to eco-cultural interdependence. There is no other intelligent choice but to discover the possibilities inherent in this change.

With over one hundred different ethnic groups, forty different lifestyle clusters, eighty-six languages spoken in the schools and more animal diversity than in other cities, Los Angeles either develops a love for pluralism and becomes *the* self-conscious heteropolitan city or it will die from social strife. It's a stark choice, which all global cities face to a degree, and one which confronts L.A. with increasing viciousness. The spectre of Belfast, Sarajevo and Jerusalem lies before it with all the consequences of denied pluralism: a 'carceral', over-armed and divided city of ghettoes. The runaway sale of small fire-arms in the suburbs shows that the population will take protection into its own hands if the politicians and civic institutions do not act immediately with more positive legislation to further minority goals and community-based economies (a proposal by the L.A. Green Party, 'Cooperate L.A.', printed here as an appendix, shows one suggested approach). If nothing substantive is done, the next round of rioting may turn into a paramilitary rebellion, as many have predicted, led by the one hundred or so gangs that now terrorize small districts.

In the 1980s it became a journalistic cliché that Los Angeles had finally 'come of age and reached maturity' because its economy had grown into a complex mixture of mutually supporting sectors and because a few new cultural institutions were designed by 'world-class architects'. But a balanced economy and several good museums and concert halls do not in themselves make a mature, whole city. Only a change in consciousness and political will towards a radical inclusiveness will do that – a new antipodal ethos which looks two ways at once, towards the particular individual rooted in an ethnic situation and towards the entire Earth community, including animals.

*(2) Frank Gehry's Snake Light, like his fish lights and the buildings, connects us to nature in an abstract and veiled manner.*

This is a book on architecture, not a sermon on doubly-coded politics; yet political and social issues form the essential background to the building. As for the architecture, a few Los Angeles designers have shown a creative opening towards a way of building that manages to be inclusive without being condescending. Frank Gehry, Morphosis, Eric Owen Moss, Frank Israel and a host of other designers have begun to fashion a hetero-architecture which suggests ethnic pluralism without naming it, and includes various taste-cultures without piling on the Corinthian columns and Latino quotations. They have done this through an architecture of analogy, wherein a variety of materials and forms imply cultural diversity and a few enigmatic shapes represent our connection to nature (fish and tree images) and culture (binocular and boat buildings). This abstract representation is one of the most vital languages of architecture shared with other designers around the world.

Here lies another lesson of Los Angeles which is perhaps as hidden as the profligate animal kingdom. It escapes the usual categories of architectural criticism and the ways in which we think about style, yet another unwanted gift. It is this: a living language of design comes and goes, today it jumps around the world unpredictably and is picked up and dropped for reasons which are not altogether clear. Many social and cultural explanations can be given in retrospect for why such a vital language grows or declines, but when it is developing fast, at a high creative pitch, then it is a form of social discourse which is fundamentally spiritual.

I am as surprised at these words as I hope the reader is, for one cannot argue that the architects discussed here are involved in any spiritual quest, or have any religious agenda, or perhaps even training. Nonetheless, I believe it to be the truth of any creative, avant-garde movement with a new and developing language: the life of forms in art, as Henri Focillion called it (or a living, surprising and inventive language of architecture) is a form of spiritual praxis. This truth is perhaps hidden even from the creators themselves.

An exact reproduction
of Michelangelo's "David"
is being carved from a
plaster cast of the original
to replace the one which
was toppled during the
recent earthquake.

CHAPTER ONE

# SELF-CONSTRUCTION
# THE ERSATZ AND THE 'REAL'

People have been coming to California since the eighteenth century in pursuit of a better life and in search of their possible new selves. Just as America attracts foreigners escaping from their past, looking for a more open way of living, California attracts Americans re-escaping for the second time, as the East Coast and Midwest fill up or exhaust their lands of opportunity. Within the state, Los Angeles is the center for self-rebirth and, before looking at its architecture, one has to focus on the various created 'selves' – both ersatz and real – which give it a distinctive character.

L.A. is perceived by outsiders as the place for getting ahead, a conceptual tabula rasa, a level playing field where competitive positions are more equalized than elsewhere. Whether true or not, the perception of this openness and opportunity becomes a self-fulfilling prophecy as it pulls in more and more people on the move; *homo movens*. It attracts more different ethnic groups, more various foreigners, more Koreans, Salvadoreans and Iowans – more pure difference – than any other place in the world. There are precedents – New York at the turn of the century, Shanghai in the thirties – but as the sprawling center of a Californian magnet it has now become the most differentiated of all cities.

Yet it is true that most large cities fabricate variety and are also mechanisms for sustaining difference. Individuals have always left the countryside, or towns, and migrated to the metropolis to find a new identity, to overcome a past, to seek a fortune; a truth recognized by nineteenth-century novelists, such as Charles Dickens, and twentieth-century sociologists. This much is agreed, but it creates a major question mark. Although the self-made man is a well-recognized type, there is deep confusion about his character. Is he a good thing, an industrious, well-rounded cosmopolite, or a nouveau-riche and fraud to be pitied and snubbed; the backbone of the industrial city, or its destroyer?

Anton Chekov, T.S. Eliot and Herbert Marcuse, to name three who might agree on nothing else, deplored the cosmopolite, the parvenu, the fabricated type, and his collective expression, the 'uprooted

*(4) Three miles of plastic trees were planted on Lincoln Boulevard and lasted until East Coast jibes led to their uprooting.*

*OPPOSITE: (3) Forest Lawn's Michelangelo – the 'exact reproduction' is exactly like the original except in every respect.*

(5) *Boy's Town Vernacular, Le Notre Mansardic carried through at the miniature scale of a converted bungalow.*

(6a & b) *Ripple Witch is one of many sub-cultural styles that has a large following in L.A.*

masses'. But these types and dynamic classes are at the same time the life-blood of any fast-changing city, especially the capitalist city which depends on the energy and wealth-creation of an ambitious set of individuals and groups on the make. Is their creativity and uprootedness to be celebrated, or condemned?

The question is also expressed as a problem of consistency, the contradiction between new identity and old style. In Britain and Anglo-Saxon parts of America, it is sometimes expected that as soon as one makes it economically and professionally, and as soon as one fabricates a new persona as, for instance, Lady Margaret Thatcher has done, then one buys an olde-lifestyle and a Ralph Lauren homestead. Such contradictions are normal and have been traditional since the sixteenth century; perhaps they existed in ancient Rome – perhaps they are eternal. Certainly ersatz, the substitution of one identity for another stems from the symbolic nature of the human condition, the fact that reality itself is mediated through symbols, and the truth that all symbols are themselves substitutions.

Leaving aside, for the moment, the question of how we judge ersatz, we can say that self-invention invents a new city, or rather many images of one, and it also creates another city type – the recluse, the romantic, the urban dweller who works at being authentic, 'real' and sincere. Naturally he is not enamored of his counterpart. Let us talk in stereotypes, since the city creates them: both the cosmopolite and the avant-garde artist, both the quick-changing socialite and the bohemian, are basic urban characters who dislike each other yet perhaps need each other. Both are self-created and both legitimize their lifestyle by pointing out their superiority to the other.

Individuals who flock to the big city intuitively know that the self is partly self-constructed through interaction with others, by trying out new languages and attitudes; in short, by entering new social situations. Existentialists and post-modern psychologists have been pointing out these facts for some time. The 'social construction of reality', or SCR as Walter Truett Anderson calls it in *Reality Isn't What it Used to Be*, has become an accepted truism of contemporary thought as much proclaimed by the deconstructivists as it is lamented by other people.[2] It has led some doubters to wonder if any solid personality exists, if there is anything that is not socially constructed or if there is any real self underneath all the language games and social masks.

Los Angeles is where this self-doubting becomes extreme, since no single way of life, belief system or culture dominates. Space and time are cut up and reconstructed differently every few years, with increasing speed. Bean fields become Beverly Hills, actors playing president become President. If the city, any city of over a million, represents the idea of liberation from small town conformism, from the constraints of fitting into one or two well-worn grooves, then Los Angeles seems to be the city of endless possible selves, the place where frictionless personal transformation can occur, the arena of ultimate do-it-yourself-self-construction. Ben Franklin was obviously from Los Angeles, so too Horatio Alger, Bob Stern and Madonna. The former Princess Pignatelli, that masterful self-constructed fabrication who has changed almost every part of her body including her smell (aromatherapy) would obviously, if L.A. had an aristocracy, be queen of the city, especially now she has lost the title she created through marriage, by that other phenomenon of self-transcendence, divorce.

But there are other modes of transformation, other ways of responding to the libertarian carnival of *almost-anything-goes*. One is shown by an architect.

*LEFT: (7) Frank Gehry as Toronto Maple Leaf Goalie: ostensibly used to promote his new line of curved-wood chairs, on which he is sitting. The image of the hockey player gives Gehry one more persona in his widening number of roles (which include acting 'Frankie Toronto' etc).*

Frank Gehry, who (has changed his last name from Goldberg and his familial roots from Toronto, Canada) has turned the ubiquitous deconstruction-reconstruction into an enjoyable language and, in the process, become the quintessential L.A. architect. He has discovered a method of self-construction without guilt, a way of overturning categories of building and living which is honest, relaxed, improvisational and informal. I will have more to say about this style of 'en-formality', the way it is transforming Los Angeles in positive directions, but quite obviously it is a reaction against the glitz and ersatz which are so much part of the background scene. Yet, at the same time, it too is self-consciously invented. Indeed, as I hope to show, one of its virtues is an expressed artificiality, the creation of an off-hand manner that appears natural to L.A. As Oscar Wilde warned, being natural is a very difficult pose to keep up; the L.A. School of architects has to work hard cultivating the careful accident, the deft collision, as hard as the classicist works at getting things straight. Even the avant-garde and authentic have to labor on their SCR.

Hollywood is obviously the industry for fabricating and polishing different selves, or at least their simulacra. If this Babylon realized its sublimated metaphysic, it would turn greater Los Angeles into thirteen million individual districts since its stars and personae become themselves through developing one aspect of their character into the brand image, the personality trait which everyone can identify. Barbara Streisand is as different as it is possible to be from Lucille Ball. The fact that movie stars inhabit interchangeable mansions in 90210 (as the Big Zip is known) shows that Hollywood's metaphysic is, however, more apparent than real and like most large industries it is targeted at a more unified image – Middle America.

Nevertheless, Hollywood Inc, like L.A. as a whole, is an agent of self-transformation. The American Dream is to become someone different, someone else, to go to sleep a pauper and wake up a prince, and part of the magic of the place is that these feats of psychic change, or lucky breaks, have happened to individuals here more often than elsewhere. The Land of Opportunity has until recently, until the Defense Department started to run down, focused on Southern California, and no place is as opportunistic in pursuing the myth.

Myths becoming true so fast for so many (if not everyone) can be very disorienting, like a boom-town that changes road-signs every year. 'What is the true self I have constructed?' or, as the more sophisticated version has it, 'how do the multiple selves fit together?'

'Child selves', 'parent selves', as social psychologists call these constructs, 'ideal selves', 'tentative selves', 'friendship selves' – there seem as many selves as there are social roles.[3] Family man in the morning, city-type during the day, surfer in the afternoon; or as Karl Marx put his ideal: Renaissance-Socialist man, hunter, fisherman and, in the evening, 'critical critic'. If, as he also said, tragedy repeats itself as farce, then Helen Gurley Brown's Cosmo Woman 'having it all' is one contemporary version of the ideal type.

As more and more Angelenos pursue multiple careers, they may become more and more unsure of who they really are. Much contemporary cognitive science reduces the self to a mere compilation of SCR's, denying there is any more unity or wholeness to a person than that created by feedback, by limitation of roles – by exhaustion! You are your CV plus memory, that's all.

This reductivism need not concern us; it is a figment of academic thinking, but the danger to which it points is very real. The archetypal Angeleno is pulled and pushed in many directions, motivated from within by the success-ethic and from without by so many opportunities for self-development that he may lose the thread of his life. Internal autobiography and recounting one's history would help overcome the schizophrenia – indeed the multiphrenia – except so many refugees to L.A. want to forget their past. Hence the landscape begins to take on aspects of a psychic explosion, a profligate variety that reflects the extreme L.A. passion for individuation, the longing to be oneself and as different as possible from the other thirteen million individuals (while remaining a bit like them in minor respects).

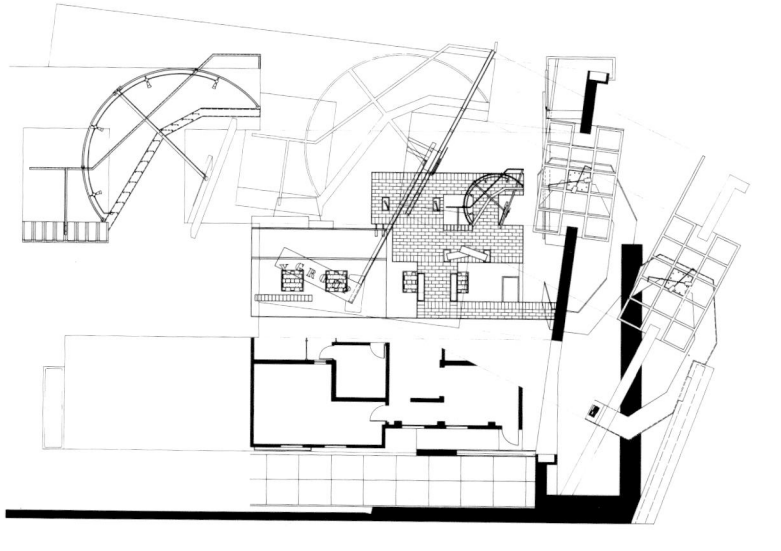

*PAGE 20 TOP: (8) Frank Gehry, Spiller House, Venice, 1981; PAGES 20 and 21 BOTTOM: (9, 9a) Eric Moss, Gary Group, Culver City, 1988; ABOVE: (10) Frank Israel, Virgin Records, Beverly Hills, 1991. 'Real Architecture' of heavy metal, exposed studs, fractured plumbing and rusting technology counters the pretty and the phoney with a bracing dose of hardware.*

CHAPTER TWO

# THE HETEROGENEITY OF LOS ANGELES

What makes Los Angeles' architecture so distinctive, so recognizably itself? Is it the background sprawl, or the foreground Pop, or the open-air living or some combination of these? Most visitors are struck by an intangible quality that defines Los Angeles as a place, some elusive feeling which makes it different from its south-western cousins such as Houston. It certainly is not the downtown cluster of forty-five skyscrapers, or the ten or twelve smaller such clusters which have sprung up on former urban villages. These, as many have said, are reproduced all over America, and now the Far East – nothing distinctive there.

What about accepted clichés? 'Many suburbs (and exurbs), in search of a city'? – but today there are countless 'edge cities'; or a 'collection of theme parks', as Charles Moore would have it? Orlando, Paris and Tokyo are nearly the equal in commercialized fantasies, but theming hardly defines their peculiar quality; 'Los Angeles, capital of the Third World'? What about Hong Kong, Bombay and Mexico City – almost equal economic powers which mix primary and tertiary economies, the extremely rich and poor. The problem with such encapsulations is not that they are not true, for each one illuminates something special about L.A., but rather the reverse, that they are all true – a paradoxical condition for any city which is big, old and dynamic enough.

As the typical urban agglomeration becomes more mature and tops ten million people, all generalizations become more provable. Thus the most convincing characterizations are those such as Edward Soja's: Los Angeles is the quintessential post-modern city of contrasts and contradictions – 'It all comes together in L.A.'

The evidence for this proposition exists on entirely different levels (economic, political, social, aesthetic) and the wealth of this ontological difference is itself a mark of maturity. There are eighteen urban village cores, one hundred and thirty-two incorporated cities and thirteen major ethnic groups which create three different kinds of layer, while the multitude of languages spoken in its schools cut up the cultural territory even further.

*OPPOSITE: (11) Hetero-architecture liberated by food, Frank Gehry's Rebecca's, Venice, 1986. Diversity of material, imagery and construction underscore the multi-ethnic, eclectic cuisine. (Michael Moran)*

Economic diversity increases the difference: L.A. is the nation's largest manufacturing location, the greatest concentration of high-technology industries (at least until the military-industrial establishment retreats) amid, paradoxically, artisan industries such as jewelry-making, furniture, clothing and movies. Sectoral divisions also fragment the population: Los Angeles is the major Pacific center of post-industrial and Post-Fordist production. Like a well-balanced eco-system, no single industry dominates. The economy is totally mixed. (Shall we say, following the ecological paradigm, it has a climax-economy?)

This heterogeneity, at all levels, is both excessive in Los Angeles and typical of the world city. London, Rome and Tokyo are also hybrid agglomerations which allow their originating village structures to remain an imprint for later diversity – but none, it seems to me, is so characteristically heteroglot. Even New York City, with its two thousand and twenty-eight different city blocks, each one dedicated to its own 'mania' as Rem Koolhaas calls these fabricated identities, seems homogeneous by comparison.[4] If the 1940s mayor, Thomas Dewey, called New York not a 'melting pot' but a 'boiling pot', then that makes Los Angeles, as a form of food, a simmering, spread out pizza with all the extras. As we will see with the L.A. School of architects, and such restaurants as Rebecca's, eating places constitute a leading building type (11).

With the Justice Riots of 1992, or whatever they should be called, it is evident that extreme heterogeneity can amplify conflict. The blacks and the Koreans, like other ethnic groups in Los Angeles' past, compete for territory, jobs and power, and this continuous struggle directly affects the architecture. It leads not only to a defensive, inward-looking building but, stylistically, it shapes architecture in two ways: either towards greater and greater heterogeneity and eclecticism; or towards more and more subtly articulated abstraction. Either way, the polyglot reality is a pressure on building, forcing the L.A. School towards its two main modes; what I will call 'Analogous' and 'Representational' modes of heterogeneity (13). Significantly, another 'L.A. School' was also formed in the 1980s, this one of planners and geographers – including Allen Scott, Ed Soja, Mike Davis and Michael Storper – was also concerned essentially, if not exclusively, with post-modern issues of heterogeneity.

Los Angeles' status as a mosaic of mostly Third World cultures is well known, but needs summarizing. It has the largest Korean metropolitan district outside Korea, Mexican metropolitan area outside Mexico, Filipino district outside the Philippines and Vietnamese district outside Vietnam, and it is second in such ratios with the Chinese and the Japanese populations. Beyond this, it has major concentrations of Salvadoreans, Indians, Iranians and Russians.[5] With Latinos, Jews and WASPs the largest minorities in this minoritized place, it is more fitting to see the area as a set of countries – like Europe – than a traditional, unified city. An ethnic map alone gives it the crazy-quilt pattern of a simmering Europe before World War One (12a). Significantly, ethnic divisions are almost equalled in potency by lifestyle differences.

If one adopts the cluster categories of market research companies such as Claritas, which divide Americans into forty lifestyle consumption groups, yet another set of divisions and enclaves emerges, somewhat overlapping with ethnicity[6] (12b).

In Beverly Hills, a cluster termed 'Blue Blood Estates', at 81.40 per cent of the population dominates 'Gray Power' with 18.13 per cent, and the two together make this area the quintessential enclave. Many Americans even know it by a zip code, that of the television program called '90210'. There are several other ethnically mixed cluster areas – Bel Air, Palos Verdes, Mission Viejo – and a few are even gated communities with armed guards, such as Rolling Hills. But whether the identity comes from inherited ethnicity or chosen lifestyle, the effect is to divide Los Angeles up into village-sized fragments, what I would distinguish as enclaves of exclusion (Rolling Hills) from enclaves of desertion (the black area of Watts). In addition there are two more distinct cultural types, what I would call 'multiclaves' to signify their heterogeneous identity. There are mixed multiclaves of transitory activity, such as Culver City, or semi-permanent balance, such as Westwood or Downtown L.A.

It is worth emphasizing, because the heterogeneity suddenly increases after 1960, that Los Angeles has been diverse since its foundation as a pueblo in 1781. The forty-four who took the site over from the Gabrieleno Indians numbered two Spaniards, two blacks, eleven Indians and twenty-nine mestizos (a mix of Indian, black and European).[7] Ever since then there has been a struggle for power and ownership, with the land divisions first formed by the fifty-five Ranchos (or ranches). These cuts were followed, more or less, by the townships and main roads and then later by the ethnic and lifestyle clusters. It is instructive to compare these maps of ethnicity, lifestyle

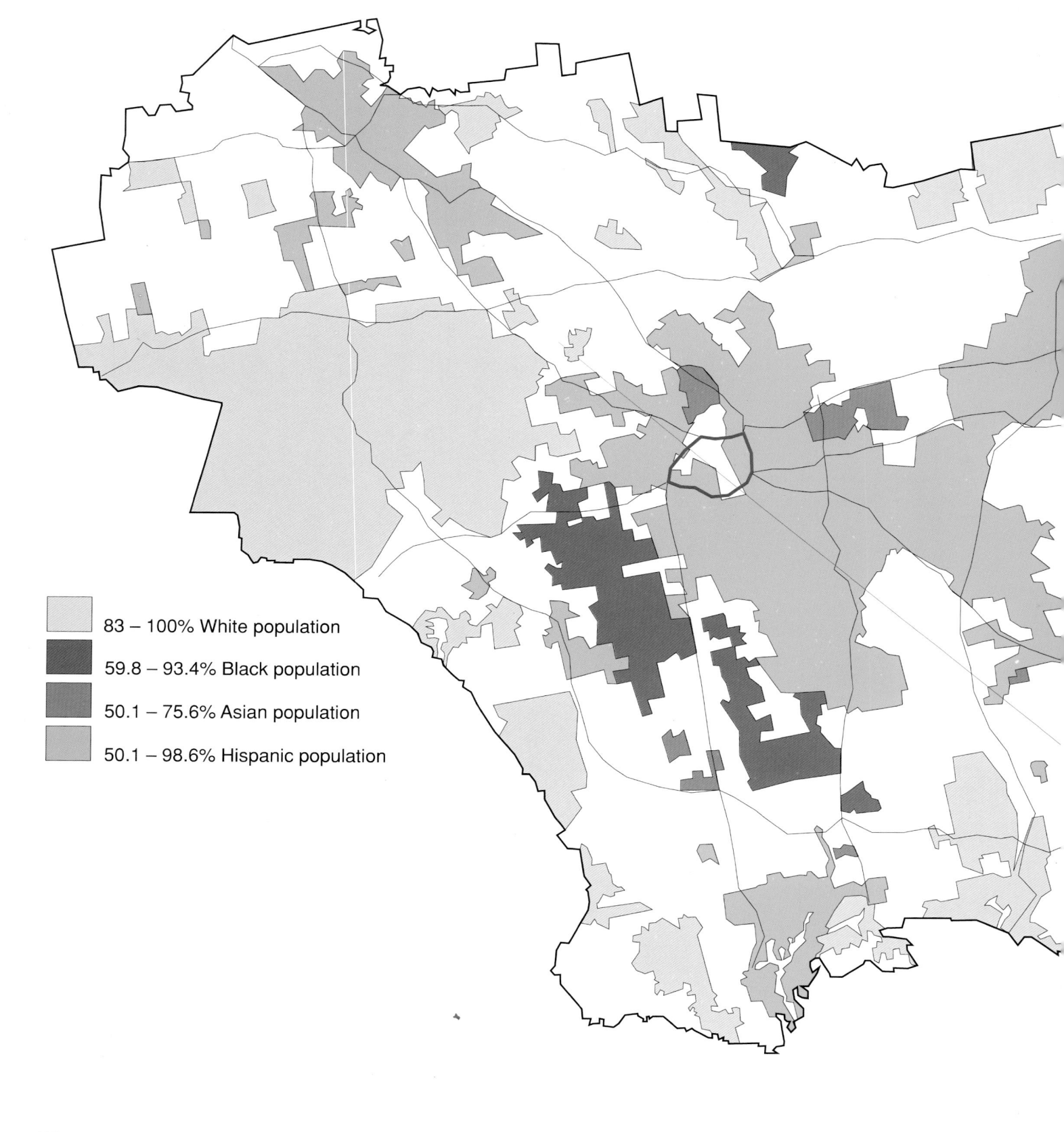

**(12a) ETHNIC MAP**

*This shows the four major ethnic divisions. Based on 1990 census data analyzed by Eugene Turner and James P Allen, Department of Geography, California State University, Northridge. (An Atlas of Population Patterns in Metropolitan Los Angeles and Orange Counties, CSUN, Northridge, CA, 1991).*

Legend:
- 83 – 100% White population
- 59.8 – 93.4% Black population
- 50.1 – 75.6% Asian population
- 50.1 – 98.6% Hispanic population

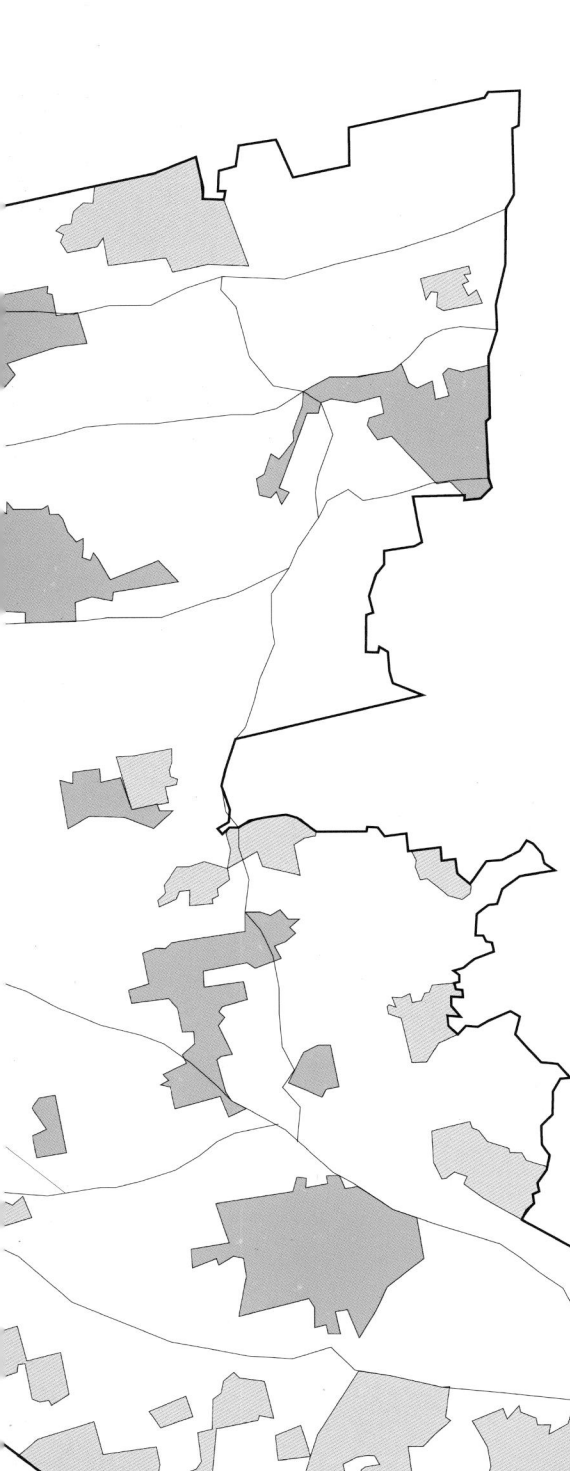

## LOS ANGELES COUNTY

| | % of total pop.1990 | % change 1980-90 |
|---|---|---|
| **TOTAL** | **100** | **18.5** |
| **Non-Hispanic white** | **40.8** | **-8.5** |
| **Black** | **11.2** | **5.2** |
| **Non-Hispanic black** | **10.5** | **0.9** |
| **Native American** | **0.5** | **-5.4** |
| American Indian | 0.5 | -7.1 |
| Eskimo | – | 64.5 |
| Aluet | – | 95 |
| **Asian and Pacific Islander** | **10.8** | **109.6** |
| Chinese | 2.8 | 161.4 |
| Filipino | 2.5 | 121.8 |
| Japanese | 1.5 | 11.3 |
| Asian Indian | 0.5 | 136.1 |
| Korean | 1.6 | 139.9 |
| Vietnamese | 0.7 | 118.1 |
| Cambodian | 0.3 | 884.4 |
| Laotian (incl Hmong) | – | 161 |
| Thai | 0.2 | 119.5 |
| Hawaiian | 0.1 | 28.5 |
| Samoan | 0.1 | 48.3 |
| Tongan | – | 151.4 |
| Guamanian | 0.1 | 67.6 |
| Melanesian | – | 77.8 |
| **Hispanic-origin** | **37.8** | **62.2** |
| Mexican | 28.5 | 53.1 |
| Puerto Rican | 0.5 | 9.3 |
| Cuban | 0.5 | 3.6 |
| Other Hispanic | 8.3 | 120.8 |

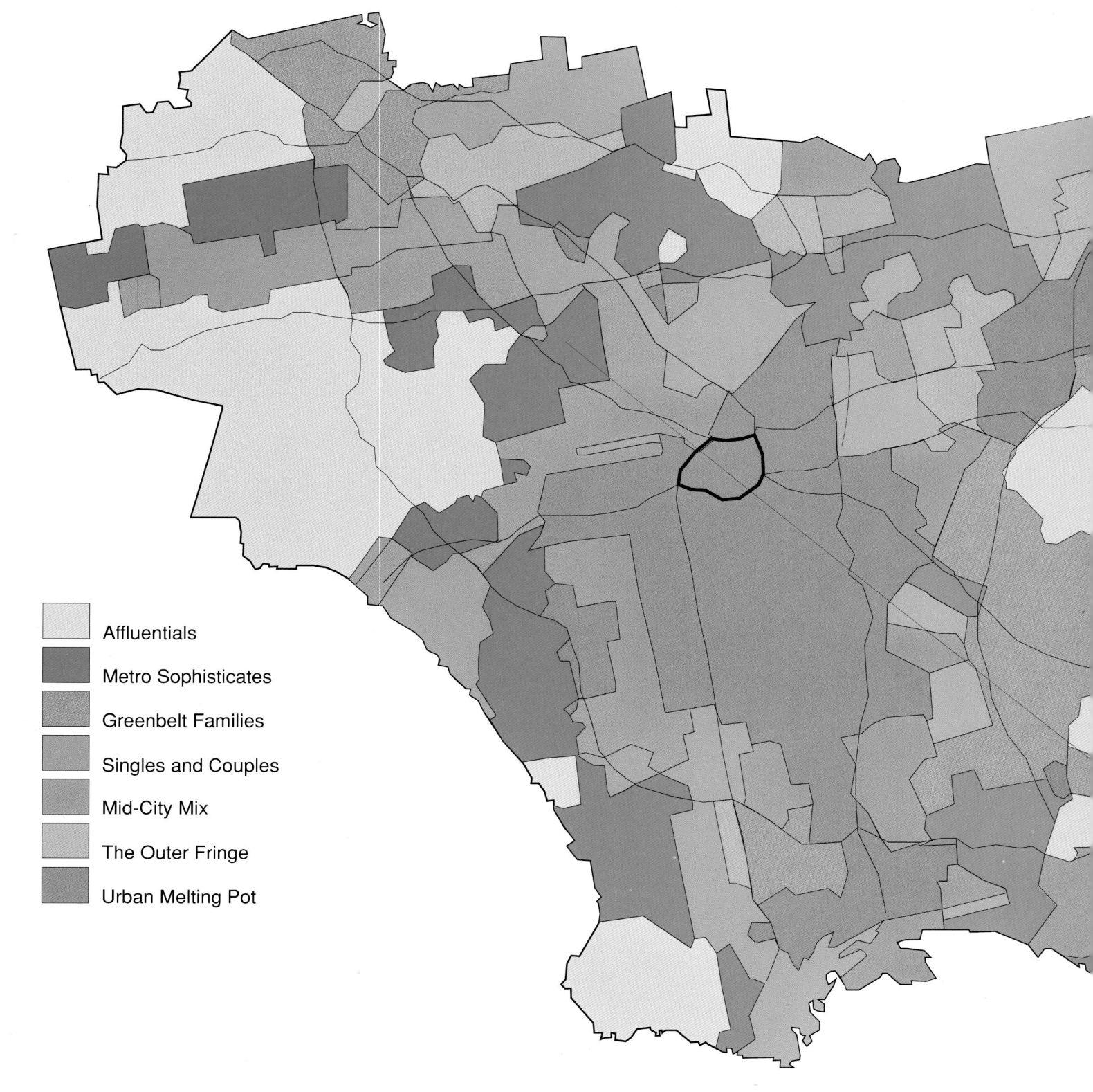

**Affluentials**

**Metro Sophisticates**

**Greenbelt Families**

**Singles and Couples**

**Mid-City Mix**

**The Outer Fringe**

**Urban Melting Pot**

## (12b) LIFESTYLE CLUSTERS MAP

*This shows where people who have the economic independence choose to live. The fact that 'birds of a feather flock together', when they have a choice, underlies this geo-demographic analysis by Claritas. A brief description of their lifestyle categories – mostly based on consumption patterns, voting records and census data – shows a different way to conceive of social grouping than the usual ethnic mapping (which it includes). In fact immigrants, as they melt into a genealogical culture, often change a given identity for a chosen lifestyle.*

## Affluentials 11.25%

The most affluent neighborhoods characterized by peak socio-economic status, college-plus educations, executive/professional occupations and conspicuous consumption levels. $100,000-plus incomes and personal wealth representing over two thirds of the city's total.

## Metro Sophisticates 17.37%

Less affluent than Group 1, these neighborhoods display similar attributes of success. Densely populated, with fewer children and a higher level of double incomes, they emulate their travel and spending patterns.

## Greenbelt Families 15.01%

The newest minority, also known as the nuclear family. They live in neighborhoods removed from city centers, in spacious single unit accomodation, and include high concentrations of native-born married couples with school-age children.

## Singles and Couples 15.36%

Predominantly young, white-collar singles and mixed couples living in dense, rented multi-unit housing. They are generally educated and upscale, with high concentrations of students, night trades, divorced, separated and foreign born. They have few children and their life-styles are active.

## Mid-City Mix 13.95%

Dense, urban, middle-class neighborhoods with duplex rows and multi-unit rented flats built over thirty years ago. They are characterized by high concentrations of foreign-born, singles, widows, elders and increasing numbers of emergent, mid-scale minorities.

## The Outer Fringe 12.77%

Contains the far-suburbs, outlying towns and rural areas. These neighborhoods consist of middle-class families, with mixed clerical and skilled blue-collar workers living in affordable houses.

## Urban Melting Pot 14.27%

Contains the least advantaged neighborhoods with concentrations of minorities and single parents living in aging, multi-unit rented housing. This group is characterized by high-school educations, blue-collar and services occupations, low incomes and perennial unemployment.

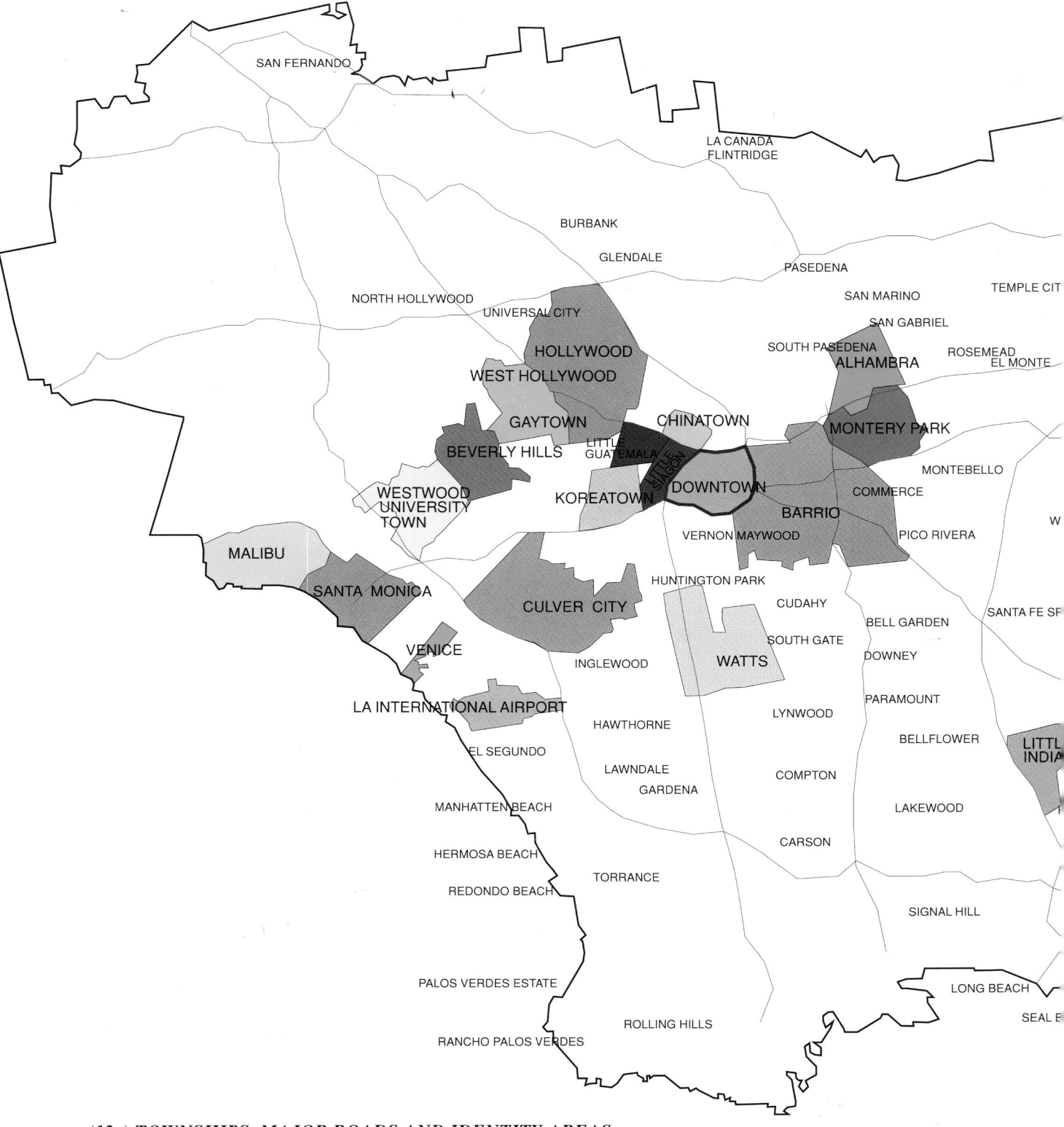

**(12c) TOWNSHIPS, MAJOR ROADS AND IDENTITY AREAS**
The somewhat arbitrary pattern of townships and roads follows the layout of the orginal Ranchos, which in turn were based on the acquisitions of large landowners. In this sense the pattern of Los Angeles is built on a series of contingencies which are continually reinforced and repeated. The identity areas, however, are recognizably distinct because of social, ethnic and functional determinants. As a mixture of physical artefact and socially constructed cognitive area they are relative to culture and only semi-permanent, but no less important for that. There are many more identity areas than the twenty shown, but these are the most commonly mentioned.

WIN PARK

EST COVIN

HAMBRA HEIGHTS

LA HAMBRA

PARK    FULLERTON        PLACENTIA

ANAHEIM

LA PALMA                    VILLA PARK

ARDENS                ORANGE

STANTON

GARDEN GROVE

WESTMINSTER
LITTLE SIAGON

SANTA ANA

FOUNTAIN VALLEY

and township with a third – what could be called 'identity areas' (the Barrio, Watts, Koreatown, Little Tokyo, Little Philippines, Little Saigon, Little Guatemala, the Gay District, University Town, Beverly Hills and Chinatown (12c).

This shows what our intuition tells us: Los Angeles is a combination of enclaves with high identity, and multiclaves with mixed identity and, taken as a whole, it is perhaps the most heterogeneous city in the world. If we could measure the variety of businesses, building types and ecologies, the total heterogeneity would be even more unparalleled. The ecological variety of foothills, beaches, plains and fast moving traffic adds to this, and is one reason that films, with their diverse requirements, continue to be made here.

### *ARCHITECTURAL IMPLICATIONS – PERIPHERY AS CENTER*

There are strong architectural consequences which flow from this heterogeneity. Negatively it means that no one style will, at least for long, dominate the city as a whole or command widespread assent – the Spanish Mission revival notwithstanding. Reyner Banham ended his 1972 book on Los Angeles with a chapter titled 'The Style That Nearly . . . ' made it: the ultra thin, lightweight Case Study version of the International Style, the mode of Pierre Koenig, Charles Eames and Craig Ellwood. This proto-High-Tech seemed ready to conquer L.A. and the world in the early sixties, and then suddenly fell out of favor. Why? It seemed too reductive, pristine and minimalist for the average L.A. temper, and architects such as Frank Gehry found it too uselessly time-consuming to detail and build, especially in a climate of approximate craftsmanship.

Funk architecture, the self-build DIY 'art of the woodbutcher' which had sprung up in the early 1960s in such places as Woodstock, New York or the boathouse community of Sausalito – the natural style of surfers and body-builders, and those whose appreciation of Miesian details was primitive – was much more to the point in Los Angeles. Improvisation, creativity, incongruity and iconic imagery – buildings shaped like castles, hot dogs or cameras – were locally valued more than the cerebral abstraction of modernism.

Yet Los Angeles, being the inclusive city that it is, developed oppositional movements together: the downtowns, Wilshire Boulevards and Century Cities grew along late-modern lines, while the peripheries went their own heteromorphic way. This sixties split established what has now become two architectural codes: Mies for the classes and hetero-architecture for the masses. What Gehry and others call the 'establishment' transforms the Downtown with a clutch of skyscrapers – forty new ones where there were only five in 1976 – which could have been built in any modernizing city at any time over the last fifteen years.[8] Architectural modernism, in its socially acceptable late and neo- forms, becomes the natural expression for modernization, as 'safe' architects from the East, such as IM Pei and KPF, are brought in to design their signature buildings (ironically notable for their impersonality). It's a sad story, repeated in every American city: as building commissions get bigger, more expensive and closer to the center of action, they become predictably duller, safer, more modernist. The dominant culture expresses this law of conformity with as much regularity as did the Romans, and the only exceptions are corporate headquarters where, very occasionally, someone tries something interesting.

'I'd rather be good than interesting', Mies van der Rohe said at the height of his corporate success in the early sixties, and the inversion of this proposition is almost the dictum of the L.A. School of architects, with its love of the botched but fascinating joint. Yet such oppositions are too simple with post-modern movements. The main architects of this movement – Charles Moore, Frank Gehry, Morphosis, Frank Israel and Eric Owen Moss – do have an interest in craftsmanship and perfecting details; but in very personal ways. These architects and their associates in heteromorphism, such as Craig Hodgetts, Michele Saee and Brian Murphy, have developed a very recognizable approach deserving the name 'School' (13).

Such a quasi-institution actually formed, and broke up twice in the 1980s, perhaps an ironic indication that individualism and difference – as cultural forms – often refuse to be organized and protected. In 1982 George Rand and I brought together one incarnation of the so-named L.A. School and a late, new version, persists informally as the L.A. Museum of Architecture Project.[9] It was a successor to The Silvers and L.A. 12, previous groups which also failed to last for more than a year and a few meetings. In spite of its disorganization and individualism, the L.A. School has a coherent architectural approach which is clearly recognizable to anyone who lives outside the city. For those inside the maelstrom the mutual identity is far from clear, and it is noteworthy that the very center of the movement – Frank Gehry – often disclaims an influence on his followers. Again ironic observation is in order. In the book summarizing recent developments,

*Experimental Architecture in Los Angeles*, 1991, the editors and publishers claim this tradition three times as the Gehry-schule, or 'The Gehry Kids', and three times Gehry disclaims paternity.[10]

In conversation Frank Gehry told me why he regards the 'third generation' more as followers of Morphosis than himself: they present pieces of buildings, an aggregate of chunks and aggressive contraptions, rather than a whole. But while this may have some truth, it overlooks the larger, broader commonality.[11] From outside Los Angeles, the School appears as a coherent whole, with an identifiable attitude towards heterogeneity and a common realist aesthetic even if, from the inside, it may fall apart. The first meeting of the L.A. School at the Biltmore Hotel in 1981 was punctuated by acrimony and the exit of one member in jealous despair. Responding to the press notoriety of Gehry's then recent house for himself, he muttered, while leaving: 'What do you expect me to do, put a house inside a house?'. The L.A. School was, and remains, a group of individualized mavericks, more at home together in an exhibition than in each other's homes. There is also a particular self-image involved with this Non-School which exacerbates the situation. All of its members see themselves as outsiders, on the margins challenging the establishment with an informal and demanding architecture; one that must be carefully read.

But, as Leon Whiteson points out in *Experimental Architecture*, 'this is a cultural environment in which the margin is often central'.[12] The ultimate irony is that in the L.A. architectural culture, where heterogeneity is valued over conformity, and creativity over propriety, the periphery is often the center. This the establishment knows, the developers and the *Los Angeles Times* know, because the media never let them forget it. It produces the paradox that the architects who make L.A. unique are precisely the ones the establishment refuses to hire for important jobs.

At least until Gehry won the competition for the Downtown Disney Hall, in 1988, the paradox was true: L.A. architecture prospered with its establishment marginals, its professional outcasts, its conventional iconoclasts. These oxymorons are perhaps the supreme expression of the heterogeneous background, suggesting that such a distinctive approach could only have grown in a city which quite naturally tolerates difference, inconsistency and contradiction. In this sense there is a continuum of culture from the all-accepting beach scene of Venice to the eclectic conversion of a warehouse.

*OPPOSITE: (13) L.A. Hetero-Architecture Genealogy. Architects on the left side tend to convey heterogeneity by analogy, through juxtaposed materials and images, while those on the right use more direct representational techniques.*

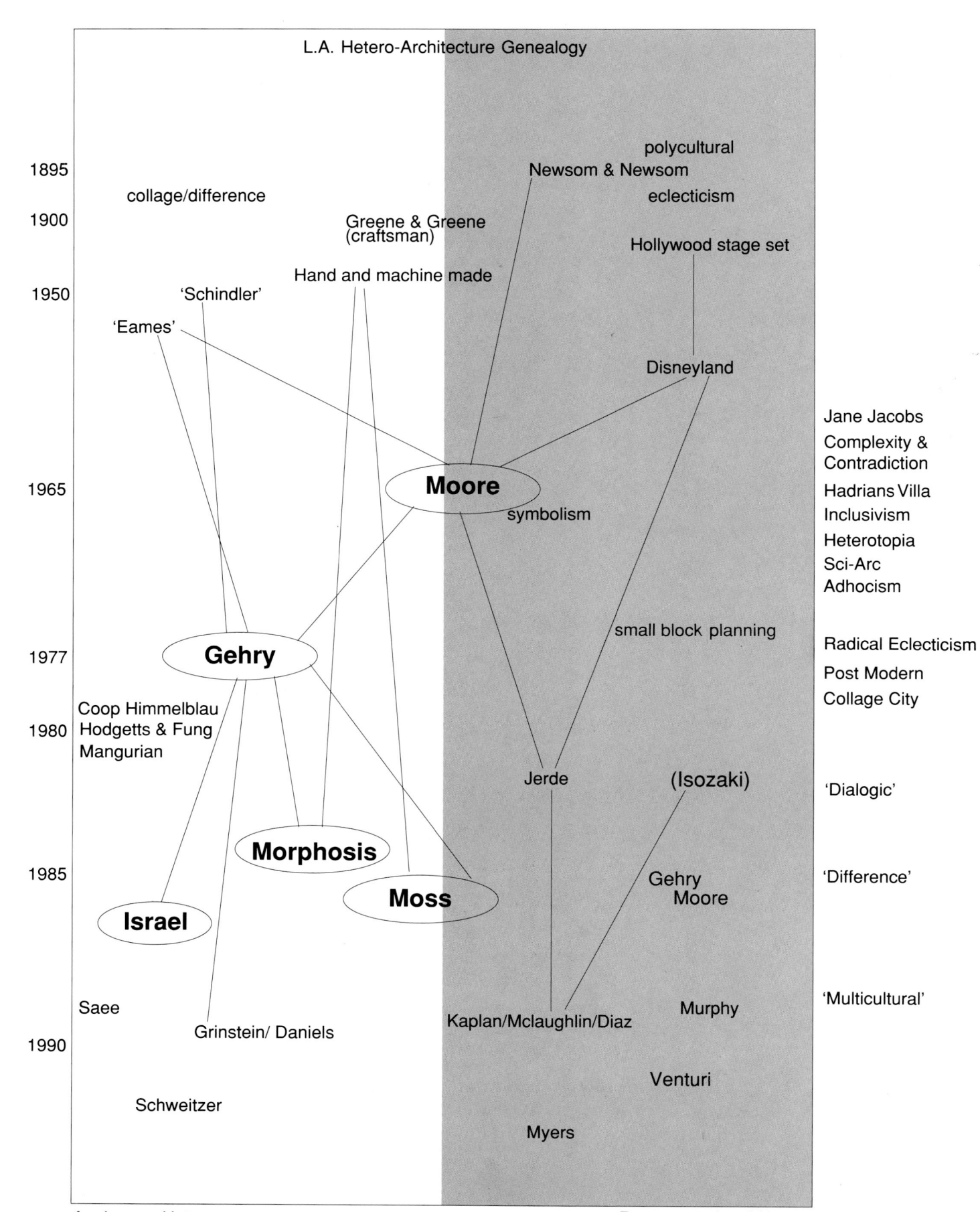

L.A. Hetero-Architecture Genealogy

1895

collage/difference

1900

polycultural

Newsom & Newsom

eclecticism

Greene & Greene
(craftsman)

Hollywood stage set

Hand and machine made

1950

'Schindler'

'Eames'

Disneyland

Jane Jacobs

Complexity &
Contradiction

**Moore**

Hadrians Villa
Inclusivism

symbolism

Heterotopia

Sci-Arc
Adhocism

small block planning

Radical Eclecticism

**Gehry**

1977

Post Modern

Collage City

Coop Himmelblau
Hodgetts & Fung
Mangurian

1980

Jerde

(Isozaki)

'Dialogic'

**Morphosis**

1985

Gehry
Moore

'Difference'

**Moss**

**Israel**

Saee

'Multicultural'

Kaplan/Mclaughlin/Diaz

Murphy

Grinstein/ Daniels

1990

Venturi

Schweitzer

Myers

Analogous-Hetero

Representational-Hetero

*(14) Newsom and Newsom, 818 Bonnie Brae, Los Angeles, c1890. Oranges and California fruit festoon the front, while wavy shingles, sunbursts, verandahs and Chinese shapes celebrate the sun culture of the Pacific Rim.*

*(15) Greene and Greene, detail of Gamble House, Pasadena, 1908. Amplified structure, downspout and Eastern allusions constitute the hybrid language.*

Everyone, except perhaps an Angeleno, can tell 'The Style That Really . . .' has arrived, because it is open, dynamic and tolerant (at least until one ethnic group, or individual, crosses and frustrates another). The tolerance, shading into anything-goes anarchism, is also why many of the architects settled here in the first place.

## PRECURSORS

The antecedents of hetero-architecture are not only the heteroglot pueblo of 1781, but subsequent invasions by different ethnic groups and individuals looking for a place in the sun. The story of this runaway development is too well known to need recounting, but less familiar – even to the architects themselves – is that an informal eclectic style (incidentally calling itself 'modern' and 'more up-to-date than Paris') surfaced in the nineteenth century.[13] The Newsom Brothers, willing to take on any mode but particularly committed to that most variegated of styles, the Queen Anne Revival, constructed some of their most creative and hybridized work in the city. On Carroll Street and along Bonnie Brae Street, both near Downtown, they built their ingenious amalgams in wood and shingle, taking up the local flora and fauna in their ornament, and making an identifiable Southern Californian language of decoration out of sunbursts, orange clusters, fish scales, waves and other regional images (14). The explicit representation may be too obvious for most of the L.A. School (except Moore and Gehry), but there are also more implicitly local themes, particularly the handling of free space, the multiple sliding partitions and the verandahs accessible by large windows. These were the inventive usages of the time that challenged East Coast decorum and the homogenization of taste. Today, when Thom Mayne attacks with concepts of 'complexity' and 'difference' the standardization of modernism, he really is an heir to the Newsom brothers, no matter if he finds their work too pretty.[14]

More obvious, and known as influences on the L.A. School, are the Greene brothers, Charles Eames and Rudolph Schindler. These are the acceptable eclectics whose pedigree is modernist enough for mainstream critics and architects to overlook their lapse into radical heterogeneity. Greene and Greene made an architecture from plumbing fixtures, rain-pipes and exaggerated tie joints, just as Morphosis and Moss were later to do (15). They would continue this Arts and Crafts commitment (what Mayne and Moss call 'authenticity') with allusions to Europe and the Far East, without worrying about unity and all the canons of exclusion that typify classicism and Modernism. With the Newsoms and the Greenes inclusion becomes an implicit goal, a subliminal assault on the idea of a single integrated language, and even a unified culture. By the early 1900s Los Angeles architects had tacitly understood the importance of 'heteroglossia', which the Russian literary critic Mikhail Bakhtin finds at the heart of certain art forms such as the novel, an idea to which we shall return.

Without explicitly defending it, because his main goals were elsewhere, Rudolph Schindler became the next exemplar of eclecticism and pluralism, at least in his handling of materials and the free plan. While consciously focused on geometrical planning, structure and more purely abstract architectural ideals, his free use of building elements at hand is particularly striking, especially in his last works of the late forties and early fifties. Here we find an opportunistic ad hoc use of any available material, on a par with Gehry's chain-link or Moss' sewer pipes. It is said that Schindler improvised because his clients were broke, and he was not much concerned with materials. As long as the spatial/geometrical idea was clear it could be made from 'crudboard' (as Reyner Banham described such high maintenance material). In any case, Schindler's free handling of cheap, varied construction was to become a key point in the later 'cheapskate aesthetic', the style of adhocism, where different systems of building are allowed their autonomy, to be celebrated as different.

Charles Eames, in his own Case Study House, pulled together an entire building from a catalogue of industrial parts, showing that modernization did not have to lead directly to purism and the International Style. So Schindler and Eames, along with the funk architects and Pop artists of the sixties, became precursors to an informal approach which would soon turn into an L.A., and even world, style.

### FIRST FORMULATIONS, 1970s

In naming this style one encounters inevitable problems: there are several, they change; architects have a constitutional dislike of style (they would rather it be a by-product of method, or personality), and there are already too many labels about. But there is no escape. If I try not to name the L.A. Style, it will slip out as a synonym, because the form-language of architecture abhors a vacuum. The only cure for one inadequate classification is another one. Accepting these

*(16) Rudolph Schindler, Tischler House, Westwood, 1949. Geometry, improvisation and informality were hallmarks of Schindler's last works.*

*(17) Charles Moore, Sea Ranch Condominium, No 1, Sea Ranch, 1965, (MCTW). Interior supergraphics, layered space, a collage of signs and honest, robust structure.*

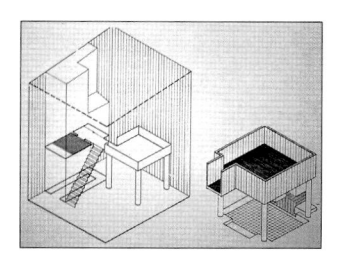

*(18) Condominium 'buildings inside of other buildings' became a method of Moore's which was then passed on to Gehry and later the L.A. School in general with their many warehouse conversions. See for instance Eric Owen Moss' 8522 (pages 69-75).*

limitations one can recall the names attached to this moving target without fixing on any of them; it was variously described in the 1970s as the 'woodbutcher's art', adhocism, radical eclecticism, post-modernism, inclusionism, technomorphism, the shed aesthetic and monopitch-coal-town.

The last set referred particularly to Charles Moore's work at Sea Ranch on the Northern California Coast, a picturesque assemblage of dark redwood sheds grouped like a little hamlet around a central court. This construction of 1965 had an industrial-vernacular flavor like an old mining town, and a romantic feeling because of its extraordinary site perched over the Pacific, but what made it catch on among architects – and be repeated across the nation – was its ingenious handling of space, imagery and wood technology. Bright supergraphics contrasted with soft bear-skin rugs and exposed flying beams in a new informal aesthetic that was at once relaxed, authentically vernacular and spatially dynamic (17-19). The L.A. Style was born five hundred miles north of the city.

A little later Moore and one of his many partners, Donald Lyndon, were to formulate a theory of place-making, current among architects at the time but distinctive in its emphasis on inexpensive materials and the use of elements ad hoc, out of context, in an improvisational way.

> . . . the first purpose of architecture is territorial . . . the architect sets out the stimuli with which the observer creates an image of 'place' . . . To build such places, often on a low budget, we like to, and must, build simply with readily available techniques.[15]

The use of 'readily available techniques' is the key idea, a notion derived from Eames. But Moore's usage was much more robust and open than the fastidious method that the modernist Eames had formulated, which is why Gehry and Moss picked it up.

When Moore moved from New Haven to Los Angeles in the 1970s he adapted the shed aesthetic to larger houses and produced a series of buildings which had his strange, slightly awkward, signature – the wandering, all-encompassing, mono-pitched roof. The two most successful were the Burns House, 1974, and a condo-minium, 1978, in which he lived, both very inventive transformations of the stucco box, the minimalist 'readily available technique' essential to L.A. mass-building. That such modes and materials could lead to very rich spaces – seventeen different shades were painted in the Burns House to bring out the layering of walls – was a lesson quickly learned by other architects, and a complex, post-modern spacial typology developed full of surprise and controlled ambiguity. It is a small step from here to Gehry's wrap-around house for himself.

Moore's other contribution was his accepting attitude towards other people's tastes, notably those of the client. Because of his avuncular personality – self-deprecating where other American architects were aggressive – Moore could make contact with different communities and gain their confidence to participate in design. Like Gehry, who followed him in this way, he was relaxed, even casual, and occasionally whimsical. This manner, new in a profession prone to machismo, was somewhat a facade, but it allowed him to institute new methods of collaborative design where people felt they could enter into expert discourse without being intimidated (20).

A case in point was the Episcopal Church of St Matthew in the Pacific Palisades, the replacement for a previous structure which had burned down in one of the typical fast-moving L.A. canyon fires.[16] The congregation was divided, ideologically and by taste, into two basic groups – high and low church. Moore, Ruble and Yudell introduced into this pluralist community various methods of participatory design, which allowed different groups to gain confidence in expressing their particular viewpoints. Some designed centralized layouts, others

*(19) Charles Moore, Sea Ranch. The monopitch coal town was an early example of what would later be known as 'Dirty Realism'. (Kathryn Smith)*

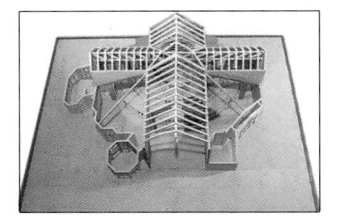

*(21) Longitudinal over central plan and intersecting structures; such mixed systems became the preferred method of Eric Owen Moss' collision composition (see pages 68-72)*

*LEFT: (20) Charles Moore designing with parishioners*

*(22) Moore, Ruble and Yudell, St Matthew's Parish Church, Pacific Palisades, 1982-84. A heteromorphic combination of central and longitudinal plans, Aalto and aedicules, exposed studs and stucco, low and high tastes.*

*OPPOSITE: (23a & b) Frank Gehry, Gehry House, Santa Monica, 1978-79. A 1920s pastiche is cut up on the inside and surrounded on the outside, creating a series of double-readings between past and present, inside and outside, vernacular and high art. Cutting and splicing past and present became, after this building, a hallmark of the L.A. School.*

more formal Latin-cross plans, while most liked the informal feeling of Alvar Aalto's Imatra Church in Finland (one of many shown in slide presentations that gauged the different tastes).

Four all-day workshops, spaced about a month apart, were set up. The first was devoted to picking the site, the next to making models of the church the parishioners wanted, a third to manipulating a kit of parts brought by the architects and a fourth to picking details and establishing an overall ambience. Inevitably this participation resulted in a complex, yet consensual, whole. Contradictions were taken as a spur to design. For instance, the low ground-hugging outside reflected those who wanted a simple parish church, while the large-scaled center reflected those who wanted a noble, almost cathedral-like, space. Dormer windows were round like the traditional rose window, but their formality was lessened by the penetration of simple vertical mullions, an echo of the wooden studs which hold up every stucco box.

The most creative result of these contradictions, and the *architectural* vindication of participatory design, was the hybrid plan: a half-ellipse, giving a centralized feeling and allowing parishioners as close to the altar as possible, and a modified Latin cross with long dormers for gables.

It is worth contrasting this motivated form-giving with the gratuitous 'ornamentalism' rampant at the time, and other vacuous formalisms including even some of Moore's work (such as his Beverly Hills Civic Center, much compromised by the client, which is basically a police station and bureaucracy done up as Verdi's *Aida*). Participation gave St Matthew's seriousness and depth of form and, as a result, the building was accepted immediately and has been well looked after by the dedicated parishioners. Heteroglossia, anchored in real social difference, is a precondition for meaning in a pluralist society.

Frank Gehry learned as much from Moore's methods and carefully careless approach as he did from the world of Pop Art and his many artist friends – Chuck Arnoldi, Billy Al Bengston and Larry Bell. In the late seventies, and with his own house conversion, he suddenly forged his second style, the one for which he is known and the fundamental basis of the L.A. Style. Previous to this some elements of the synthesis were present in his Davis House, but it was only with the freedom which came from being his own client and the impetus of other forces (such as Constructivism and the Daydream Houses of

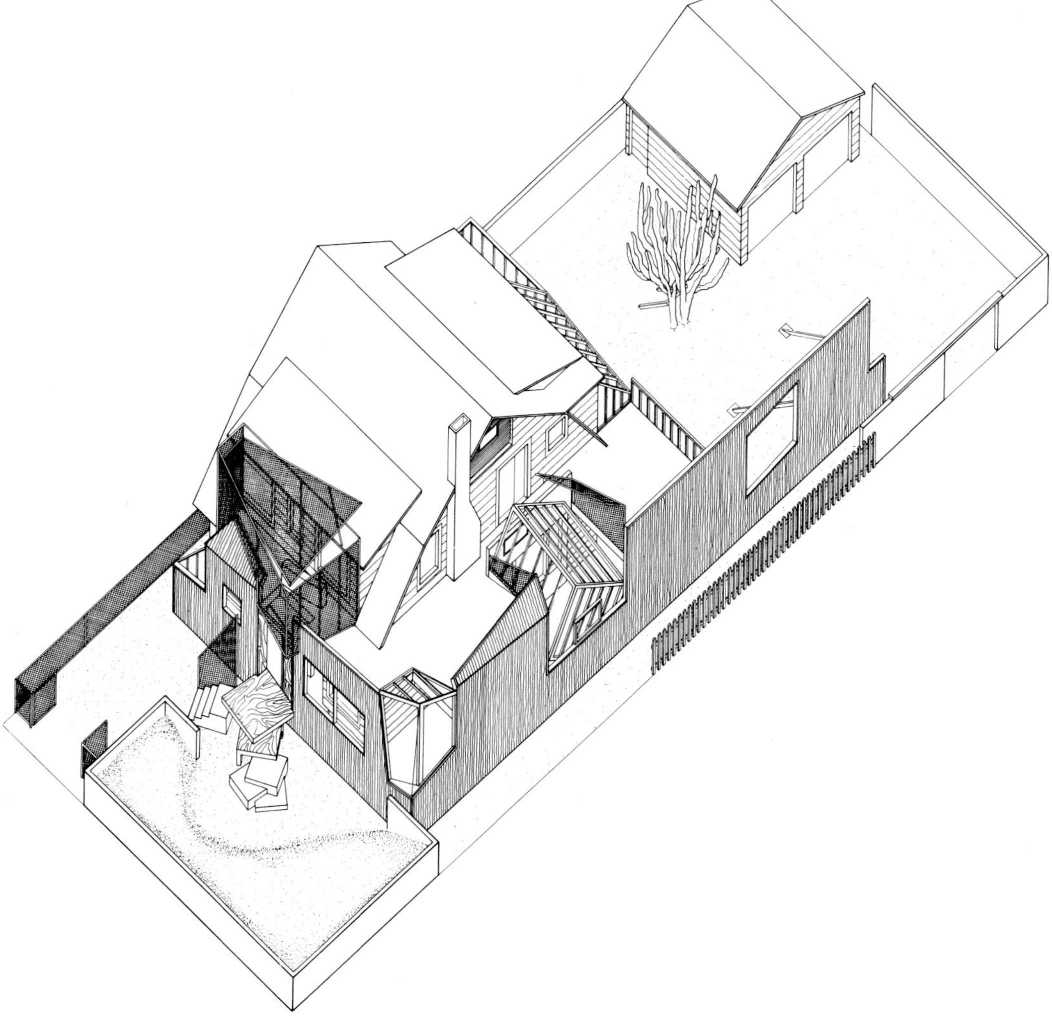

*(24, 25) Frank Gehry, Wosk*
*Penthouse, Beverly Hills, 1982-4.*
*Small block planning, the break-up of*
*a single task into a village typology*
*and a set of juxtaposed languages.*

L.A.) that he made the breakthrough and attained a synthesis. Here, to summarize the influences, is the 'wrap-around ruin' of Louis Kahn, the exposed studs and woodbutcher detailing of Charles Moore, the spatial layering and complexities of Robert Venturi, the pink-vernacular and white-picket-fence of West Hollywood, the deconstructions and excavations of SITE, the tough materialism of Modern architects and – his very own – 'cheapskate aesthetic', the corrugated siding and chain-link fence used as flying wedges (23a & b). They sectioned the old house like a butcher slices a chicken.

Architecture would not be the same after this, either in L.A. or elsewhere. The building as a calculated manifesto was taken up immediately because it corresponded to a shift in mood – towards the informal and expressionist. Even the mainstream *Time* magazine understood the point and amplified what, by now, had become a media event – leading to that rancorous outburst I have mentioned. With this building the L.A. School fell apart at the very moment it coalesced into an identifiable style.

Frank Gehry has commented on his curious relationship to other Angeleno architects, both in *Experimental Architecture* and in conversation. As someone who was overlooked, or slighted, by the previous generation of architects and critics, Ray Kappe and Esther McCoy, and someone who never developed friendships with his followers, such as Thom Mayne, he could only find deep appreciation, oddly enough, from an unlikely ally on the East Coast.

> When I began to find my style there simply wasn't much of a support system [in L.A.] for anyone trying to do something different. There weren't a lot of people I could talk to. The established firms jealously guarded their turf and considered the few of us who were trying to innovate as interlopers who threatened their sense of security. The man who did most to change this mean situation nationally was Philip Johnson.[17]

Johnson and Tim Vreeland toured the Davis House and since that point, in the mid seventies, Johnson has been a tireless champion of Gehry and his so-called *schule*.

While his own house marked the real breakthrough in design, Gehry's most radical heteromorphic architecture was to come. There were several projects in the early 1980s, such as the Whitney House, which fractured a single commission into many separate pieces – each in a different material, color and image. These amalgams looked as if they belonged to different architects, all sharing the same funk aesthetic. The most successful built works of this period were the Loyola Law School, Wosk Penthouse, Temporary Contemporary, Aerospace Museum and Norton House, most of them additions to, and transformations of, existing buildings.

One of the great strengths of the L.A. School and hetero-architecture in general is its ability to work with and against the existing context at the same time. Virtually all the best work of Morphosis, Israel, Moss, Saee and company is a conversion – typically of a warehouse. Some architects are at their best with an impossible site and an existing structure to modify, the typical conditions prevailing on the margins of Los Angeles practice. A greenfield site and tabula rasa, the ideal conditions for modern architects, does not often bring out their creativity. Instead, interacting with an existing structure and strong client produces very personal, rooted architecture.

A case in point is the Wosk Penthouse, an addition of eight or so pavilions to the top of a Beverly Hills apartment block which is, below, a large stucco box. Here is the small block planning, such a hallmark of post-modern (and Leon Krier's) urbanism at the time. Here is the juxtaposition of different discourses – vernacular greenhouse, blue (not golden) dome of Nero, corrugated shed, etc – all playing off the vigorous and fruity taste of the client, the painter Miriam Wosk. Her strong colors, Mexican tiles and Art Deco zig-zags are at once absorbed and allowed autonomy. No voice dominates in this dialogue. Gehry provides a set of themes and background, and she provides much of the detail, ornament and finish (24, 25).

Even more important, because it was small block planning for a semi-public task, is the Loyola Law School addition, built over a long period. Because classical law provided the pretext, Gehry could modify the Greek temple, Roman palazzo and Romanesque church to give a veiled equivalent of classical, legal precedent. Placing several such forms in opposition, building them from cheapskate materials and without the customary ornament, he managed to fit in both with the adjacent slum and the fastidious skyscrapers of downtown Los Angeles. In the center of his scheme an open-ended piazza, punctuated by different volumes, creates the public realm. In some respects this is the most public architecture recently built in

*(26, 27, 28) Frank Gehry, Loyola Law School, Los Angeles, 1981-84. An informal combination of Mediterranean building types, none of which is explicitly represented: the ultimate in suggested heterogeneity by analogy. Unfortunately, for security reasons, the scheme turns its back on the street, and cuts itself off from the reality of city life with a wall of metal. Visually and symbolically, however, it relates to the adjacent towers of the Downtown as well as the local neighborhood.*

Los Angeles, for it provides a pedestrian precinct in a variety of modest but expressive modes, and one with which the varied population can identify – Hispanic, black, Anglo, Jew and certainly those from Mediterranean cultures (26,27,28).

Familiar cultural and ethnic signs are almost, but not quite, present, thus allowing the user a certain latitude of interpretation and appropriation. This is not the universal grammar of Modernism, the idea that we can only unify a pluralist culture by speaking in abstractions. Rather it is a subtle form of eclecticism in which particular voices can find a response. The difference between these two positions over the question of difference is the key. The first holds that multiculturalism must lead to the equivalent of Esperanto, or else a zero-degree neutrality; the second that heterogeneous cultures can be acknowledged through analogues of difference, and even traditional forms and meanings where they are sufficiently veiled and transformed.

## REPRESENTATIONAL HETERO-ARCHITECTURE
## THE 1980s

An indication of where the debate on representational architecture had reached in the early 1980s is Arata Isozaki's Museum of Contemporary Art (MOCA), built after an interesting power struggle between artists, architects and patrons.[18] Placed in the center of a downtown redevelopment mega-project of stunning banality – the cynical L.A. triumph of greed and uptight taste over culture – it was born through a loophole fathered by creative financing and the mandatory 'one per cent for Art'. The rest of the mega-project, the other ninety-nine per cent, was expensive and dull enough to warrant building a museum to take people's eyes and mind off the sordid background and the method by which it 'won' a limited competition. Fittingly, the bankrupt architecture has been followed by the bankruptcy of the architect, who left the country in a hurry.

The controversy over the museum itself focused on whether it should be a neutral shed for art – Gehry's 'Temporary Contemporary' for MOCA showed how fitting this could be – or something more challenging. In the event Isozaki produced an understated essay in post-modern representation, fusing recognizable pyramids, Renaissance garden and Palladian windows with veiled allusions to garden trellises (in the green steelwork), and the south-west (in the rich red sandstone – actually from India, but which looks Arizonan). In plan and section he included veiled allusions to Eastern and Western mystical traditions, but no one would know this unless they had been told. The significance of the building was in the masterful control of spatial surprise, and the fact that a major architect had finally been chosen for a prime downtown commission and, for my argument, the fact that representational allusions had been carried through with enough finesse to inspire and validate more (29).

The major visual problem Los Angeles architects have faced is brought on by stereotyping and exaggeration. Hollywood and the brash Pop known as 'Vernacular California Crazy' set the dominant tone and then Disneyland turned it into a formula, watering it down in the process. All these set such a powerful standard of cliché that it made understatement more welcome than usual. In fact, architects such as Moore and Isozaki tried to continue overstatement and ambiguity in a new way, and Moore defended Disneyland for its urban creativity in an article published in Yale's *Perspecta*: 'You Have to Pay For the Public Life'.[19] His own Disnoid public realm for the Beverly Hills City Hall is also disappointing because the public does not give it the intense use it needs, and its imagery is overblown. But the formula – the commercialized pedestrian precinct – has achieved a few notable results.

The most authentic, architecturally, is Gehry's Santa Monica Place, 1979-81, a shopping center recently complemented by Johannes Van Tilburg's Janss Court, next door. This is a decent version of post-modern urbanism which fills out a city block, thus holding the street lines, and it provides mixed uses and an interior promenade. The representational architecture – with its gables and banding – is trite, but at least the heterogeneity reflects the mixture of functions and contradictory urban requirements (30).

In the same line of pastiche eclecticism, but more up-market, is Kaplan McLaughlin Diaz's Two Rodeo Drive, a simulation of nineteenth-century street architecture and the real Rodeo Drive to which it is attached. Like Disneyland's Main Street, from which it is derived, the facades are diminished replicas, but they are shrunk to nine-tenths the original, not Disney's three-quarters. Miniaturization is a way of gaining virtual control, or cerebral power, over an environment, as anthropologists remind us, which is perhaps why it has also become the formula for commercial ersatz and the ubiquitous L.A. mall. Control, stereotyping and sales go together; the shopper wants an environment which is safe and predictable. At

*(29) Arata Isozaki, Museum of Contemporary Art (MOCA), Downtown Los Angeles, 1982-86. The first important Los Angeles public building by a major architect – an indication that the city was finally 'coming of age'? After this building The New York Times, Time, The Atlantic etc took up the theme 'L.A. Reaches Maturity'.*

*(30) Johannes Van Tilburg, Janss Court, Santa Monica, 1989-90. Housing over commerce, a movie theatre, arcade and older buildings – the sensible piggyback solution holds the urban pattern with mixed uses.*

(31) Kaplan McLaughlin Diaz, Two Rodeo Drive, Beverly Hills, 1988-91. Representational heterogeneity representing the nineteenth-century European streetscape and adjacent Rodeo Drive – without any comment.

(32, 33) The Jerde Partnership, CityWalk, Universal City, 1989-93. Tight pedestrian streets opening onto a circular piazza – like Charles Moore's Piazza d'Italia – provides just what Los Angeles does not have: continuous pedestrian streetscape with no gaps.

Two Rodeo Drive a single building is cut up by an interior cobblestone walk, open to the sky like a Parisian alleyway, while the exterior is themed as twenty-five separate shops. The heterogeneity and pedestrian urbanity are welcome, but one has to pay quite heavily for the public realm in terms of the kitsch – the period detailing and bronze carriage lamps (31).

Undoubtedly the master of this commercial genre is Jon Jerde who has made mid-ersatz into a high/low art. The popular Horton Plaza in San Diego, 1986, established his practice as an international leader in turning shopping centers into eclectic urban places. After his Westside Pavilion in Los Angeles, and a few less successful malls elsewhere, he formulated a strategy known as 'urbanopolis', the not surprising idea that people like to walk in tight streets and squares while they shop, and the fact that this truth can re-urbanize the most powerful building type of the last twenty years, the shopping mall.

Up and down the flatlands of Los Angeles one can find versions of this new building type trying to be born. There are mini-malls trying to be theme parks and village streets; and theme parks, such as Knottsberry Farm, trying to be shopping centers. All of them are attempting to be something else, and exulting in this otherness and phoniness. At Knottsberry Farm, as at Disneyland, stucco facades are constructed with pre-aged cracks and spalling surfaces, thus memorializing the Spanish Mission crumble, while anticipating what is known as The Big One, the great earthquake to come. I once stumbled across a real wedding ceremony there with rented guests (sic) dressed up in nineteenth century finery.

If Two Rodeo Drive is a pastiche of an adjacent phoney, the Real Rodeo Drive, then the architects KMD have made nothing, either ironic or playful, of the fact. Jon Jerde, with his CityWalk project now under construction promises something more (32, 33). Having researched Los Angeles with the idea of finding out what makes it unique architecturally, he came up with the notions of transience, energy and the spirit of unplanned vulgarity. Speaking to the reporter Amy Wallace, he said:

> L.A. is not a fixed thing. It's a moving target, an elusive energy psyche that is not physical . . . [filled with] dumb stucco boxes and 'Look at Me!' signs . . . L.A. was never a designed city. It was kind of a business transaction gone amok . . .[20]

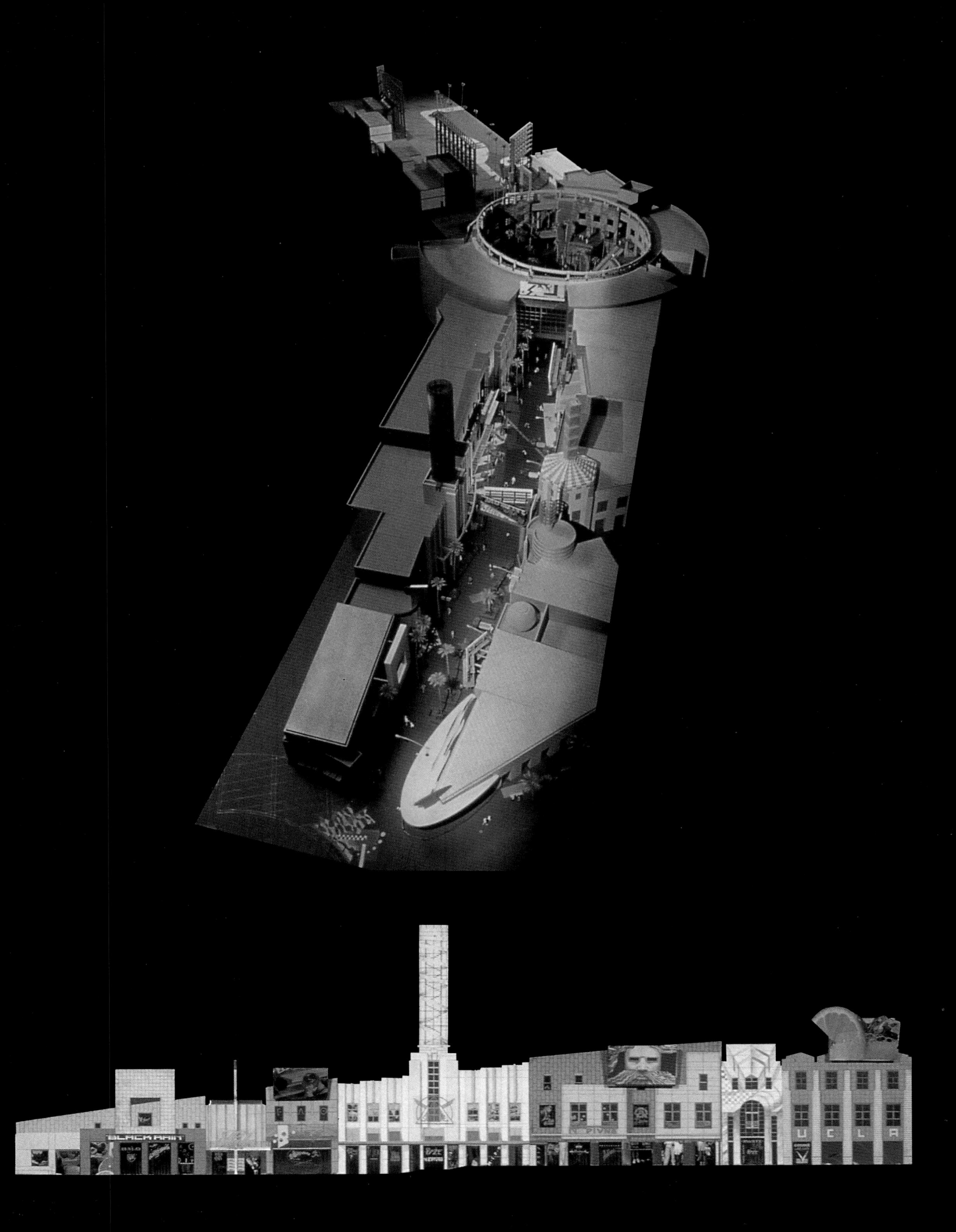

The enticing question for Jerde, and the film empire of Universal City, is how to simulate the business transaction run amok, the peculiar combination of hyper-profits and hyper-fantasy. Their answer is surprisingly realistic. Inspired by eye-catching buildings and billboards on Sunset Strip, they are asking the prospective tenants of CityWalk to produce something weirder, brighter, uglier and more experimental than usual. None of your good-taste mall – 'more vulgarity'! Inevitably some are rejected because they are not outrageous enough, probably the first example of counter-contextual contextualism in the world.

When Los Angeles planning laws institutionalize 'wacky elements' and 'out-of-keeping-it-has-to-be-more-shocking', then you know the city has finally reached a certain self-understanding of its heterogeneity, however crude.

Jerde's partner in charge of the scheme, Richard Orne, is as direct as a cowboy about some of the motives: 'What I would hope for is a lot of bad taste . . . A kind of, "screw you, I'll do whatever I want" [attitude], which is exactly how Los Angeles was formed'.[21] Graffiti will be welcome in parts and, just to keep the tenants wacky enough, selected 'hotspots' will catalyze the timid: 3-D billboards with moving parts, a seventy foot neon totem pole featuring a huge King Kong dangling from one side and other stereotypes of movieland. The only things kept out of this simulation are real poverty, crime and unplanned spontaneity.

Controlled spontaneity will be hard to achieve, but not impossible, and however unreal the political pluralism and false the image, at least the thorough-going eclecticism is welcome. Architecturally the result promises to be much more vital than Disneyland's, and over- rather than undersized. It will be one and a half real scale (32,33,34).

The advantages and disadvantages of this kind of urbanopolis are quite clear. Negatively, it is the old problem of the theme park and its mono-functional hedonism. 'Entertaining oneself to death', the spectre of the rat pressing the pleasure buttons wired into his head until he drops from hunger, became a symbol of escapist America in Reaganland (Disney-on-the-Potomac). The 'mallification' of the country, theme park combined with shopping center, 'entertainment architecture' with commerce, became the successful formula at the price of robbing both functions of an embedded context where other realities might intrude. The developers of CityWalk enthuse over their new building type, the 'festival marketplace', and the way it pulls in

*OPPOSITE: (34) The Jerde Partnership, CityWalk, with its 'idealized reality', the controlled spontaneity of drainpipes, tangled electrical conduits, shouting billboards, palm trees and glitz – all without crime. The leasing director, Tom Gilmore, says:'I don't need the excitement of dodging bullets to go there'. It's extraordinary that bullet-free shopping should be such a high priority, but such is the fear of mugging and rape in the old downtowns, that it leads directly to the triumph of the controlled environment, the mall and its simulated street life. Real reality is shut out for the ersatz of managed bad taste. And this in turn leads to the reaction and taste for 'Real Realism', heavy metal, 'honest aggression'. CityWalk is in the middle of a masterplan for Universal City, the ultimate safe city in the city. Idealized Reality has finally been isolated from Real Reality.*

three different types of audience – 'diners, shoppers and fun seekers'. But, in the sense that everyone is here to be entertained in a distracted sort of way, it is really monoculture playing at variety, not real heterogeneity.

Nevertheless, the eclecticism is there and it was partly based on interviews with the surrounding inhabitants and a participatory design which produced many of the amenities they wanted – among other things, an art gallery and night-time UCLA extension center, which will keep the place alive longer than the ersatz Main Street of Disneyland (or even the actual Downtown). So, as is often the case in post-modernism, false simulations lead to some real (as well as false) benefits.

There are exceptions to this ersatz eclecticism, a few who understand the real thing. If an outsider, Isozaki, opened the door to post-modern representation then another one, Robert Venturi, again showed that it could be carried through at a high level. His Medical Research Laboratory for UCLA very skilfully transforms the adjacent vernacular – the heavy dumb box dedicated to health – into something urbane and amusing (but nonetheless strict and rational). Here finally is a building which plays with multi-colored brick, stone and concrete – the grammar of the campus – in a new way (35, 36). The volume expresses its utilitarian packaging in its repetitive, flat-chested window-wall, making a new visual virtue out of the flush detailing and then, when necessary, inflects at the corner to allow a walk-through. Here is a building which makes the workplace into an aesthetically charged location – as we will see, a prime characteristic of the L.A. School. Perhaps its greatest contribution to Los Angeles is to turn the monofunctional office into a convivial place where anything might happen and bring pleasure back to work.

*OPPOSITE: (35, 36) Venturi, Scott-Brown, MacDonald Medical Research Laboratories, UCLA, Westwood, 1989-92. The huge medical building of the campus is modulated urbanistically into three parts, plus a garden and corner walk-through. A second research lab will enclose the garden court. The typical anonymous medical factory – the loft building – is articulated rhythmically with UCLA colors and signs, the slight variations signifying differences in labs versus offices, window-seat areas and special corner rooms. A large-scale ornamental arch – appropriate to the road and distant view – contrasts with the small-scale limestone ornament and colonettes, meant to be perceived up close when the second building is complete. The building has the heroic straightforwardness of an industrial loft combined with the delicate touches of a palazzo.*

CHAPTER THREE

# THE L.A. STYLE IS FORGED
# EN-FORMALITY

While a representational eclecticism was camping up mini-malls all over L.A. with gables and colorful peaked hats 'à la Aldo Rossi', the fractious L.A. School turned more ascetic, difficult and tortured in response. The former were dayglo and effulgent with their architecture of 'Have a Nice Day', so the latter became more sullen with their architecture of heavy metal and chain-link. Ironically, the style Thom Mayne christened 'Dead Tech' became the mode for eating out and actually enjoying oneself, as if one's taste-buds were sharpened by raw concrete and rusting steel.

Dead Tech, that is, High-Tech after the Bomb, or ecological catastrophe, signified a new, sophisticated attitude towards modernism coming out of Sci Arc (Southern California Institute of Architecture), the avant-garde school of architecture that Mayne's partner, Michael Rotondi, took over in the 1980s. Whereas modernists had a faith in industrial progress, signified by the white sobriety of the International Style, the post-modernists of Sci Arc had a bitter-sweet attitude towards technology. They knew it brought pollution, knew that progress in one place was paid for by regress in another, but nevertheless still loved industrial culture enough to remain committed to the modernist impulse of dramatizing technology. 'Technomorphism', the young critic Aaron Betsky called it, reminiscent of the same phrase used to describe 1960s Pop Artists and techno-fantasts such as Archigram.[22] But whereas Archigram was still, like the modernists, optimistic about a liberating technology, the L.A. School conceived it in more ambivalent terms, sometimes celebrating its sado-masochism (the trussed-up heavy metal construction glorying in its gusset-plates), other times lamenting its transience (the melancholic rusting steel member exposing its dark red fragility to the outside street).

Morphosis (Mayne and Rotondi) started this tradition with their 72 Market Street, a Venice restaurant finished in 1985, and developed it further with their Angeli's Restaurant, 1985, Kate Mantilini's Restaurant, 1987, and Club Post Nuclear, 1988. Some called this the 'Post-Holocaust' style (after Ridley Scott's 1982 cult movie *Blade*

*OPPOSITE: (37) Morphosis architectural drawings, 72 Market Street, Venice 1983-85. The red melancholic glow of this painting/architectural drawing evokes high-tech after the L.A. catastrophe. Raw concrete, steel members and a mechanical contraption – here the earthquake reinforcement of a central column – became the structural formulae for Californian cuisine in L.A. after this restaurant.*

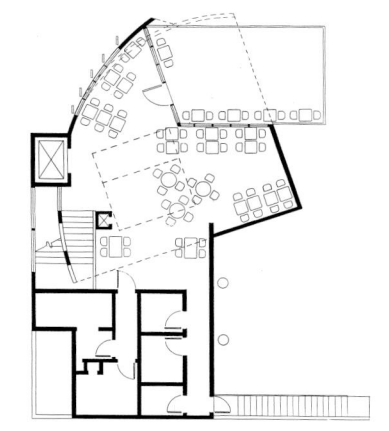

*Runner*) and it is once again appropriate to connect films, stage-sets and social attitudes to Los Angeles architecture. For some reason the style caught on for those serving the most healthy and exotic 'California Cuisine' – that mixture of French Cuisine Minceur, simple Japanese tastes and eclectic add-ons from India and Mexico. Punk architecture usually meant smart food. David Kellen designed the FAMA and (with Josh Schweitzer) the City Restaurants in 1989, in an expressionist version of the Gehry aesthetic; Schweitzer himself darkened its mood with the black and rust-framed Border Grill, 1990; Elyse Grinstein and Jeffrey Daniels inflected it in ethnic directions with their Chaya restaurants of the late 1980s and towards a pop-constructivism with an eat-in-billboard for Colonel Sanders (38-39a); and Michele Saee became the master of the genre with his Japanese Restaurant, 1989, Angeli Mare, 1990, and Trattoria Angeli, 1987. Saee, who worked for Morphosis, continues what he calls the 'rustic and elegant' in his restaurants, and such a combination reminds us that the L.A. style is not all *Sturm und Drang* with sheet metal.

Yet the rusting corten steel is what first hits us at Trattoria Angeli, jutting out from the corner just above eye-height – two aggressive bronze-colored beams (40) which hold up the dissolved corner like left-over scaffolding and, since they look like props added to shore up voids left by an earthquake, add to the sense of transience and catastrophe. The Angeli sign also angles menacingly onto the sidewalk, while a blank wall of corten steel (shielding the inside diners and meant to be an L.A. billboard) is really an advertizement for the tough, urban landscape. The inside has major hallmarks of the L.A. School – exposed bow-string trusses of the converted ware-house, an extraordinary (and useless?) mechanical contraption known as a cantilevered bridge (going from nowhere to nowhere) and cantilevered lighting fixtures which resemble metallic reptiles about to strike. The sinister technomorphism is, however, countered by the normal familiar accoutrements of an Italian restaurant (41).

So the mood conveyed by such buildings is an ambiguous mixture of aggression and hedonism, sadism and restraint, functionalism and uselessness, self-promotion and withdrawal – a calculated informality that I would call 'en-formality'. It is hardly as simple or straightforward as it appears, and it has appeared in so many buildings, not to mention restaurants, that we can really speak of a new convention, a shared aesthetic and attitude. At first approxima-tion it looks close to the well-known Japanese philosophies and

*OPPOSITE AND ABOVE: (38, 39, 39a) Grinstein/Daniels, Kentucky Fried Chicken, North Western Avenue, 1988-90. En-formality adapted to fast-food. Roadside architecture of pop icons, disjunctive signs and clashing forms is turned into a high art version of itself in cool grey tones. An extra-large square window and curving wall that peels away marks the roadside, along with Colonel Sanders. The interior space modulates the strong exterior light and noise of the road producing a suitable mixture of realism and quiet.*

*(40) Michele Saee, Trattoria Angeli, West Los Angeles, 1987. The anonymity of the white stucco box, and former carpet warehouse, is shattered by the dark explosive corner, at once billboard to the street and heavy metal protection for the inside diners.*

*(41) Michele Saee, Trattoria Angeli, interior. Like other L.A. School conversions, it features the building's pre-existing trusses set against fixtures and furniture that are collaged into the skeleton.*

aesthetics of Wabi and Sabi, those systems of being which tea masters and Zen monks have developed over the centuries. Emphasizing the common and rough over the fussy and decorated – poverty over luxury, silence over loquacity, restraint over ostentation, spare over ornamented, serendipity over planning – it was appropriated by the modernists Bruno Taut and Walter Gropius in their appreciation of the Japanese Sukiya style. But, as Kisho Kurokawa has argued, Wabi and Sabi are always double encoded, and include their opposite – display, luxuriance, ornament – as an undertone.[23] They are emphatically not the simple, reductive styles that foreign interpreters have made them.

In like manner the L.A. Style – or en-formality – is complicatedly informal, rough and ascetic. These qualities do predominate, along with the heavy metal contraptions, but behind them is another mood altogether. Despite everything, the architecture is friendly at heart, outgoing, open and accepting. Indeed this is the central focus of hetero-architecture: the ability to absorb other voices into a discourse without worrying too much about consistency or overall unity. That such an approach should reach consciousness with Frank Gehry, and then self-consciousness with subsequent members of the L.A. School, shows a maturity rare at a time of quick change. The information world usually dissolves these movements of shared sensibility as soon as they are formed, in a blitz of media attention, but here a common attitude has managed to develop, perhaps because of the background culture of Los Angeles. It too mixes a sunshine gregariousness, an openness to new experience, with a tough streetwise realism.

Morphosis has been instrumental in forging this melancholic style, as much in their drawings, models and personae as built work. Aloof, austere, downbeat, often unshaven, like characters in an MTV skit, they give the impression of being on the run, of living on the edge of sanity. How much this is simply the style of a whole generation, which shops at Esprit and finds in Heavy Metal a complete metaphysic, remains a question, but there is no doubt that the young find Thom Mayne's call to authenticity and sincerity – words of the Romantic period – is a welcome alternative to historical pastiche. What he means by authenticity is a 'return to basic sources', a 'presence within materiality', a 'description in the process of making' – all values evident in the thoughtful details of the work.[24] Whether it is a chair, table, lighting fixture, door handle, window blind or electric meter, the construction element is exaggerated in its material presence, much as Anthony Caro foregrounds his steel armatures.

One of the most authentic and convincing details, in this architecture of fragments, is the sculpture – yet another technomorphic contraption – forming the focus of a waiting room for children undergoing cancer therapy. Half mechanical monster with TV monitors allowing instant feedback, and half the image of a tree growing towards light, it provides a powerful source of physical interaction and enigma for waiting patients (42). Contrast it with the usual dead, anodyne reception room, or its alternative with seaside prints, and its authenticity is clear: high technology, radio-therapy, the age of simulation (which Mayne sees as the fundamental challenge) are all acknowledged, as well as the fear of impersonality and clinical professionalism. By confronting these facts directly, Morphosis has turned them into a narrative both awkward and poetic.

That this awkwardness provides a sign of authenticity in an era of slick showmanship is as certain as Gary Cooper's famous stutter, and the L.A. School – like the Zen tea master – has made an art of the carefully controlled mistake. Again Gehry's house is the exemplar, with its punched out windows and torn surfaces, very much the art of the contrived botch, and the bungle placed so delicately that it must have taken years of flower arranging.

Morphosis, in their refurbished block for the Salick Health Care Company, breaks down a pre-existing homogenized volume into smaller fragments which lean this way and that, jostling like crowded spectators for more space (43). Modernism always privileged similarity over difference, Mayne insists, as he cuts up its surfaces and contrasts materials and joints.[25] Yet the awkward juts of the curtain wall, the obtuse angles and collisions are as premeditated as any classical composition. Once again it is high architecture reflecting heterogeneity and not actual street life itself (security guards see to that). Mayne even concentrates on the traditional architectural values: the way the building touches the earth and sky, how it turns the corner and is layered in section – the drawings and models convey this commitment. So what appears at first as another essay in deconstruction is, on second glance, a sophisticated attempt at articulating difference: cutting up one building into two, and then further fracturing the elements so they symbolize heterogeneity.

(42) Morphosis, Cedars Sinai Medical Center, Los Angeles, 1988. An electronic 'tree' and 'monster' films the children who are patients and turns the waiting room into a playful jungle gym.

(43) Morphosis, Salick Health Care Inc, Beverly Hills, 1990-92. Mayne speaks of 'the notion of the way the building touches the earth and sky . . . how it defines the edge . . . how it ends ambiguously at the top and is layered . . . how the masonry starts heavy and terminates as billboard . . . [how] part of the wall escapes to define the corner, literally describing the cutting process . . . [and how] one building is weaved together as two, a dialogue with a missing link, defined as a peel'.

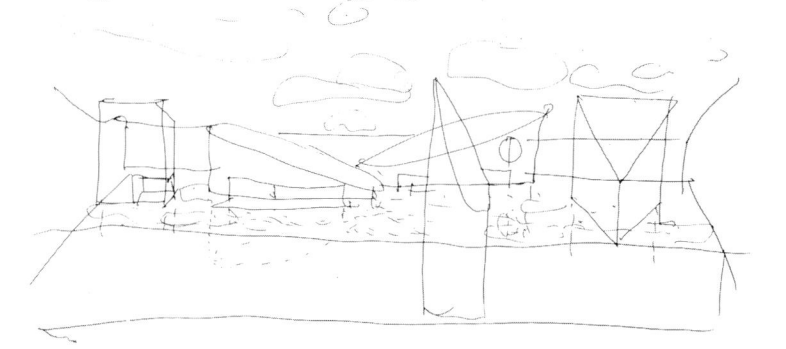

*FROM ABOVE LEFT TO RIGHT: Tea Ceremony Room, Katsura Palace, Japan, seventeenth century; Frank Gehry, Artists' Studios, Indiana Avenue, Venice, Ca, 1981; Aerospace Museum, L.A., Ca, 1984; Winton Guest House, Wyzata, Mn, 1987; American Center in Paris, France, 1993 (Josh White); Rasin Office Building, Prague, Czechoslovakia, 1994; Jung Institute, L.A., Ca, drawing, 1976.*

## THE FORMATION OF
## EN-FORMALITY

*En-formality is more than a style and approach to design, it is a basic attitude towards the world, of living with uncertainty, celebrating flux and capturing the possibilities latent within the banal. Those who enjoy informal living are not necessarily most attuned to its virtues, which require a kind of wry detachment and passion for the unexpected. These allow a designer to notice qualities hidden within an ordinary situation, or everyday material. Frank Gehry, when confronted with a piece of uptight, pristine plastic – supplied by Formica to launch a design product – threw it on the ground in a moment of frustration. It shattered and the boring homogenous material suddenly revealed some interesting shears and serrations which he then exploited in a series of 'fish' lights.*

*The bricoleur, or handyman, also stays very close to materials and whatever is at hand, improvising with his limited tool-box and restricted set of methods. Ingenuity is always at a premium, the clever transformation of one set of solutions into another. Such basic creativity is valued, even idealized by the Los Angeles School as a method, and it results in ad hoc concatenations that are clearly recognized as such. The ideal is to stay close to nature, or the products of industrial society seen as a kind of second nature. The sensibility exists in all periods of history, but it is particularly apparent in Dutch art of the seventeenth century, in the work of Chardin and in Van Gogh's famous painting of his forlorn pair of tatty shoes.*

*With the Japanese aesthetic of Wabi and Sabi and the tea ceremony, the poetic is completely conventionalized. The typical Japanese tea room of the seventeenth century was constructed from whatever materials were at hand – a branch from a nearby grove of trees, a stone from the roadside, decaying boards of boats – and vernacular techniques such as thatch, tatami mats and trellis. This ad hoc architecture looked 'natural' and as it aged the informality seemed even more an extension of the growing world. But the tea house, and its attendant ceremony, are highly artificial, stylized and edited: they follow many prescribed rules developed over time. An analogous convention has grown out of the vernacular and funk architecture of Los Angeles.*

## FRANK GEHRY AND
## SMALL BLOCK PLANNING

Although there are many precedents, Frank Gehry was the first architect to bring this adhocist method to self-consciousness, and public consciousness, with his own house completed in 1979 (23a & b). All the later hallmarks of the approach are here, from the studied awkwardness of colliding planes to the open aesthetic which includes anything to hand: an older house, picket fence, corrugated metal, an oversized cactus and tarmac for the floor of the kitchen. One can see features from former styles, such as Constructivism, but the striking aspect of the design is its unclassifiability, the way it turns the crossing of boundaries into a new recognizable image.

Gehry's other main contribution to the developing paradigm was to break up a building into a set of existing pavilions. Again there were many precedents for this idea of small block planning both in contemporary and historic architecture, varying from Greek temple planning to the schemes of Louis Kahn and Leon Krier. But where Classicists would have adopted rules of symmetry and similarity, Gehry gave these prototypes a particular informal twist, as can be seen in his first essay in the genre, a design for the Jung Institute of 1976. Here volumes are sliced, distorted in perspective and juxtaposed to accentuate difference.

That there are rules of en-formality, however fuzzy, is intuitively obvious. Anyone can recognize a Gehry design and the so-called *Gehry-schule*. Bold, flat monochromatic volumes are always juxtaposed. Windows, as in the Artists Studios on Indiana Avenue, are usually over-size and squarish. The compositional outline follows the requirements of a function – such as a chimney-flue or a plot-line – thus dramatizing brute necessity. Plywood and asphalt shingle are used 'as found', as if they were picked up off the beach and each house is a different color thereby articulating personal identity. Such primitive methods, always staying close to necessity, push the aesthetic close to the Froebel-block planning of Frank Lloyd Wright, as indeed to toy-blocks in general. This approach reached maturity with the Loyola Law School of 1981.

Soon thereafter, at the Aerospace Museum and Wosk Penthouse, Gehry added recognizable imagery to his arsenal. A Lockhead F104, iconic sign of flight, contrasts with the background abstraction: a blue dome from 'Nero's Golden House' is juxtaposed with vernacular forms, and fish, snakes and natural images begin to accompany each project. Partly this turn to abstract representation reflects the widespread post-modern movement and its intention to move beyond elitist abstraction towards an inclusive language which can reach across taste-cultures; partly it reflects Gehry's taste for the striking image used out of context to jump-shift a change in mood.

Small block juxtaposition reaches the level of high art, a form of flower arranging with building, with the Winton Guest House of 1987. Red brick volume with its chimney turret, black metal pyramid, rust plywood rectangle, grey sheet metal box, and curved limestone fish-shape are set in maximum contrast – material, color and form each marking the difference between pavilions. Can fragmentation and opposition go any further? Perhaps not with the articulation of volumes, which may be why Gehry sets off in another direction of individuation.

His latest way of breaking up the box is carried out with only one or two materials – rather than the previous four or five – and a method of slicing shapes and smacking windows onto the frame of a very compressed volume. The constricted building package once again makes a virtue of necessity – it is the cheapest way to enclose space – while the cuts and twirls give the lumpy volumes life. The American Center in Paris, now complete, or the Rasin Office Building proposed for Prague are characteristic of this dual intention. At once hard-headed packaging and a slippery overcoming of categories and building types, these strange and heavy beasts make one think: why is so much ordinary architecture merely ordinary? Gehry likes the banal site, the dumb requirement, the low budget – or is often inspired by these restrictions to wiggle his building in inventive ways, rather the way Francesco Borromini in the seventeenth century was provoked by similar limitations. Necessity and the industrial imperatives Gehry shows us, can be turned to surprising and aesthetic ends.

## MORPHOSIS AND HETEROMORPHOSIS

Thom Mayne and Michael Rotondi, founders of Morphosis, have developed heterogeneity towards a new style of craftsmanship. It is approximate rather than refined, raw and brutal rather than delicate, industrial rather than natural, complex not simple, and botched not perfected. It is one where liminal spaces interpenetrate to break down any sense of a fixed boundary, any notion of completeness or mastery. In a sense they capture a prevalent mood where technology has overwhelmed the natural and human world, a threatening state which is out of control. 'Dead Tech', 'post-holocaustic design', 'anti-humanism' were epithets they and others used to describe their method of design, but these labels failed to capture the optimistic and creative aspects of the work.

Always focused on details – how a stairway is lovingly put together, how heavy metal members can frame a chair – their designs have the presence and facticity of sculpture. In this way they transform what might otherwise have been an alienating environment into something very personal and poetic. The method, like that of the Italian architect Carlo Scarpa, with whom they are often compared, also results in the priority of the part over the whole. This emphasis on the detail – again evident in the drawings and models – leads to a studied fragmentation and also to their metaphysic. Contemporary industrial culture is seen to lead to fragmentation, the self is broken, or severely challenged by meanings which do not form any coherent pattern. This they accept and represent through complex images that combine perspective, plan, elevation and detail – all in one drawing. In fact all the L.A. School adopts this convention of superposition.

Paradoxically, by representing the fragmentation and seeing through the fabrication of every detail until it has a sensuous presence, they turn alienation on its head; they rediscover the self and the body in the presentation of small parts beautifully executed. The well-detailed part thus stands for the missing whole.

The first building where this approach is fully realized is Venice III, 1982, the third in a series of small Venice buildings that captures the funk aesthetic of this beachside area. Here materials are juxtaposed for maximum contrast: white sails shading skylights are set against sheet metal towers; asphalt shingle walls contrast with concrete slab and steel rigging. Rectangular forms break up and step down furthering the fragmentation. Material and space are layered to dissolve any sense of closure.

With the Kate Mantilini Restaurant, 1986, their work takes on a more representational note: an oculus, cut into the ceiling, has a kinetic orrery at the top and, just below it, there is a curved painting which depicts prize-fighters at work (the restaurant was named after a fight promoter). At the bottom another metal contraption describes the plan of the building on the floor: 'architecture about architecture'. From this time on the heavy metal contraption and the idea of narrative all continue as preoccupations.

As important as their buildings are the obsessive drawings, paintings and multi-material models produced by Morphosis. These are not only worthy of being put on permanent display as works of art, but they are investigations of conflicting architectural ideas. How do contradictory structures frame into each other? How does each autonomous part take over and dominate the whole? How are space and materials layered in a complex way that breaks down identity? Part diagram, part conceptual sketch, part melancholic portrayal of a lost wholeness, these artefacts suggest a complex civilization that has been dug up after it has been destroyed by a neutron bomb that has left the skeletons.

No doubt schizophrenia is suggested by these representations and one that is not romanticized but faced. Awkwardness, honesty and an out-of-control precision are conveyed – hallmarks of a technomorphic civilization that has lost its way. Is this why Morphosis became *the* architectural firm for students to emulate in the late 1980s? Do they see in the work a way of reflecting negative processes and turning them into a redemptive art?

Michael Rotondi, having left Morphosis and started his own practice, has developed the idea of improvisational design even further than Frank Gehry. For a small house for himself, he designed in tandem with the builder, responding each night with a new set of drawings to the work done during the day. As he said: 'The objective was to produce a project over a long period of time like a city develops – starting, stopping, remembering and forgetting. This results in being a heterogeneous system of related and unrelated parts. These drawings were used for construction.'

This cybernetic process of design, quite common in pre-industrial architecture and before the law profession made it impossible, results once again in extreme heterogeneity, an architecture that reflects the multiple decisions and changes of mood of any city under construction. Rotondi's work has the qualities of a sketch: like the assemblage sculpture of the 1960s, it prefers vitality and function to visual completion. It is yet one more analogue of the city of Los Angeles in motion.

*BELOW: Morphosis, Kate Mantilini, oculus and painting, 1986 (Tom Bonner); OPPOSITE FROM ABOVE LEFT TO RIGHT: Morphosis, Venice III, addition to a small house, Venice, 1982 (Ranier Blunck); Morphosis, Sixth Street House project, 1988 (Tom Bonner); Michael Rotondi, CDLT House, Los Angeles, 1987-91; Michael Rotondi, CDLT House; Morphosis, Arts Park Performing Arts Pavilion, Los Angeles, drawing, 1989; Morphosis, Arts Park Performing Arts Pavilion, Los Angeles, model, 1989.*

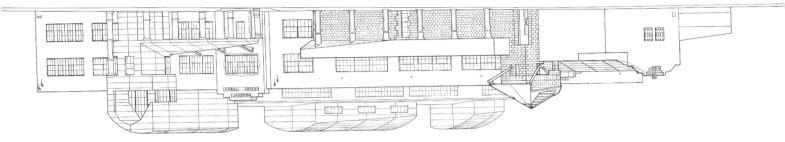

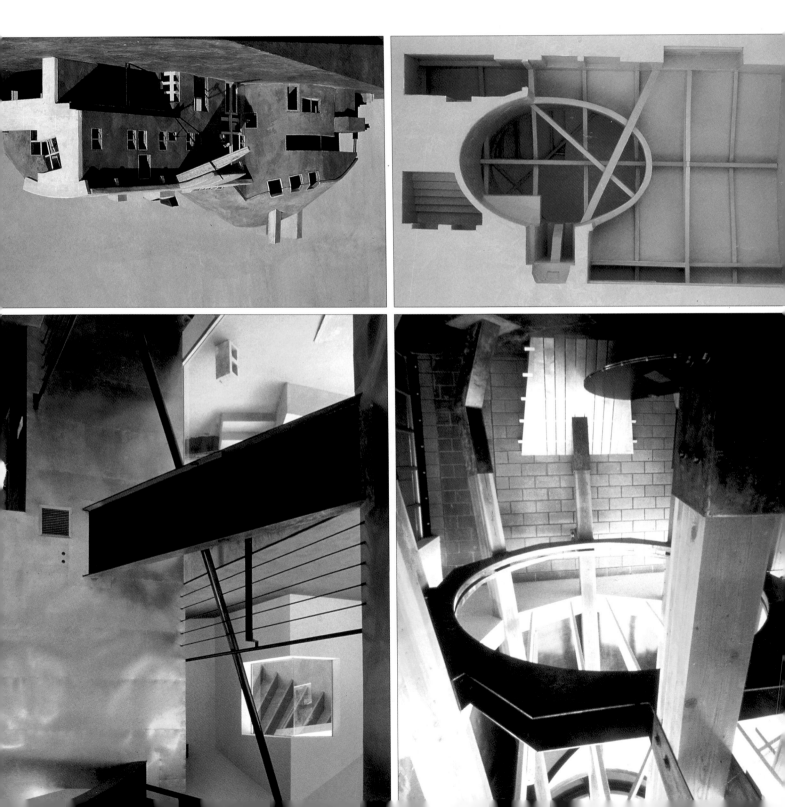

## ERIC OWEN MOSS AND THE CATACLYSMIC STRUGGLE OF OXYMORON

The abiding norms of modern architecture were simplicity, consistency and straightforwardness, all the rhetorical devices that affirmed a reductive worldview. Generations were trained in values that presumed the universe could be understood in a few basic laws and simple propositions: 'form follows function', 'less is more', 'truth to materials', 'design from inside to outside' and so on. Budding modernists were told to use only one structural system where possible and a monochromatic finish to integrate the whole. Totality and diagrammatic clarity were sought, the contingent was denied, pluralism suppressed, history abolished, memory expunged. Inevitably many architects forget the lessons. As Gore Vidal said of this period in America, it was the 'United States of Amnesia'.

Eric Owen Moss, like so many postmodernists, has inverted these norms one by one. His buildings always feature complexity and the contingent as much as they accentuate simplicity and geometry. They positively exult in the conjunction of opposed systems of thought and reality. A strong idea is set up to be partially interrupted and refuted, a bold form is presented to be unceremoniously challenged by something completely different. This gives his work an explosive energy, rather Michelangelesque in its sculptural cataclysms and contrasts. Forms wrestle with each other and shout each other down – the drama is that of a fierce argument between opposed sides who both know they are right. The approximate craftsmanship of Gehry and Morphosis here becomes engaged in a tragic struggle. Awkwardness is even more pronounced, the buildings are more robust, more quixotic, and uglier (ugliness, as it has been for a hundred years in architectural theory, is compensated by character). At times the *terribilita* becomes mannered and horrific – one wishes Moss knew when to stop elaborating an idea. But if he did, and he stopped taking chances, would his work have its energy? More than any other Angeleno designer, he makes great architecture from pushing the boundaries and the struggle of opposites. His work is the apotheosis of contradiction and oxymoron, the result of facing paradoxes inherent in the different timeframes of past, present and future.

His cataclysmic style reached maturity with the 708 House (for himself) in 1981. The giant size numbers (his address) jumps across three facades, offset by diagonal green squares, white concrete and a discordant brick string course. Baby blue polka dots run across a false pediment mocking the pretentious musculature around them. Can he be serious? No, might be his answer, no one can in a cosmos known to be both pretty and violent, ridiculous and meaningful. James Joyce, and his elaborated puns and oxymorons occupy Moss' thoughts as they do Gehry's. The time city of Dublin, or Culver City, is too big to be encompassed by any system or singular mood. His Lindblade Tower leans this way and that, shifting both to the street and the nearby freeway; off-the-peg clay sewer pipes are cut in half to reveal the real concrete structure and allow lighting fixtures. The universal and the contingent fight it out as they do in the orbiting moons of Jupiter that he admires, the ones that tumble chaotically while they also follow geometrically precise paths.

Given this predisposition to confront order and chaos, it is not surprising that two of his favorite figures are the violated ellipse and the ruptured circle. The former is evident in the Uehara House, an oval form bisected by two skewed lines and eroded to one side. 'Imperfect perfection' is the obvious oxymoron. The latter is evident in the conference room of the Gary Group. Here we find a basic circular geometry asserted on the floor, halfway up and on the roof, while intervening levels also assert the octagon, square and pyramid.

Such layerings of four contradictory geometries would drive Mies van der Rohe into another profession, but it is also true the complexity has precedents in Islamic domes and the baroque spheres of Guarino Guarini. The latter represented infinity with his heavenly complexities, whereas Moss, Culver City cosmologist that he is, represents all sorts of contingent things: the function of a conference room, the steel holders which grasp the laminated columns, the steel cone of the roof and 'the line of the perverse' (the way one requirement cuts into another and hybridizes it). Moss thus reminds us that the universe, and architectural requirements, *are* sometimes perverse, their perfect geometries are often violated by ridiculous things – or other perfect geometries.

Hybridization is also represented in the color of the Lawson/Weston House. The finish is steel troweled plaster with two colors put on simultaneously to get a kind of 'no-color', or camouflage, a distinctive tone that can be felt, not described in a chart. Here also perfect forms are violated, especially by windows which appear in the grammatically wrong place or at an angle. Perverse? Yes, but done with enough straightforwardness not to be maddening. Like Gehry, Moss knows when to play his idiosyncrasy in a dumb way, like a throwaway joke. A magical aspect to this house is the way an overall colortone unites opposite surfaces – such as roof and wall – while the unity is bisected by funny protrusions and tantalizing spaces. The simple cone and circle generate the form, but this underlying geometry is so hybridized by additional requirements that one can only feel their presence as a trace. Contrapuntal ideas are thus more veiled and subtle than before, only suggesting their previous existence as generating forces. The memory of past, present and future (for future is inscribed in the memory as projection) is thereby blended. The time city has become a house.

*BELOW: 708 House, Pacific Palisades, Los Angeles; OPPOSITE FROM ABOVE LEFT TO RIGHT: Gary Group, Conference Room, 1988-90 (Tom Bonner); Lawson/Weston House, interior of main space (Tom Bonner); Yoko Uehara House, Pasadena, model in plan, 1986-87 (A. Vertikoff); Lawson/Weston House, West Los Angeles, 1988-93 (T. Conversano); Lindblade Tower/Paramount Laundry, elevation, 1987-89.*

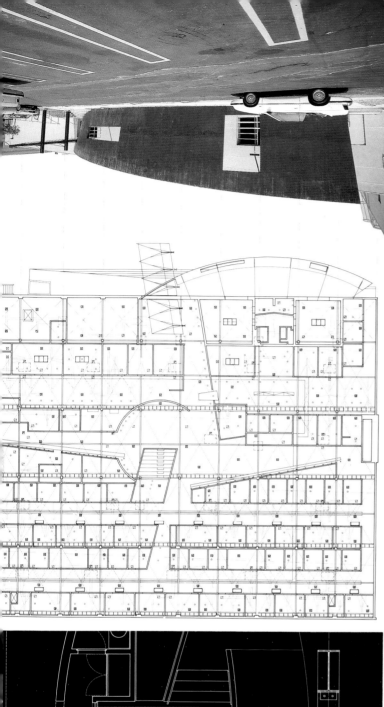

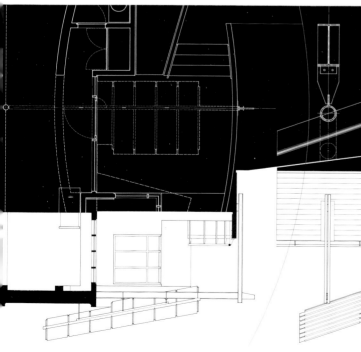

## FRANK ISRAEL AND THE REFINEMENT OF EN-FORMALITY

Partly because Frank Israel came on stream a few years after the previous designers and partly because his sensibility is more understated (and East Coast), his version of en-formality is more refined than the others. Israel is an interior designer as well as an architect, his choice of materials and colors is consequently more self-conscious and controlled than the rest of the L.A. School. With him the sketch of Gehry and Rotondi becomes the deliberated gesture. He thus pushes the L.A. Style towards a kind of system, contradicting its spontaneity and naturalness (which, in any case, are somewhat feigned).

The artifice of being 'natural' is the essence of the L.A. aesthetic and approach. It takes years of learning and unlearning; for Israel this meant a preparation at the University of Pennsylvania, Yale and Columbia (where he was taught the primitivism of early modern architecture), the Rome Prize in Architecture (where classical attitudes towards nature could be seen) and many more years of teaching at Harvard and UCLA. Education in the Los Angeles style of improvisation takes more time than a training in Beaux-Arts architecture: being natural *is* a difficult manner to learn.

Israel's retrofit of the Propaganda Films warehouse is a classic L.A. conversion in the tradition of Gehry, Moss and Morphosis. All the conventions are here: open and closed spaces alternate; figural shapes such as a 'boat' are set against an abstract grid of streets and avenues; the office-as-village once again turns its back on a dangerous and polluted street outside; white walls and concrete are contrasted with the ubiquitous bow-string trusses and other elements of the warehouse; present is set against past, monuments against background. But the contrasts are softer, the mood more lyrical and controlled than the other conversions. Indeed if one looks at the floor plan of the Virgin Records Conversion, this subtle control of the ad hoc can be immediately grasped. In this layout the office-as-village reaches its most labyrinthine and sophisticated development.

An equal mastery of the aesthetic can be seen in the Tish-Avnet office conversion of 1991. Here the angst-ridden interpenetrations of Moss become the refined balances of a Cubist painter: a sloping curved wall in yellow stucco slides in from the right to be carefully skewered by a structure of red steel beams and white sandblasted Plexiglass that looms up through the tight space pinching in close to a window-wall of dark blue squares. Juan Gris would have been happy to collage such perfectly balanced and contrasting colors and shapes. What is lost in vitality is gained in delicacy. The L.A. style is here declared a style, a loss of innocence to be celebrated, not suffered.

The Goldberg-Bean House is another case where the Mossian cataclysms have become controlled Israelian compositions of color and form. No defiant gesture is unstudied or out of control: a characteristic L.A. School drawing – combining plan, section and elevation in one rich complexity – sees to that. The sheet metal curves of the master bedroom (is the shape a vestigial Gehry 'fish'?) slide deftly under a strongly projecting balcony, while above, glowing in two shades of rich dark red, are redwood battens and cedar plywood stained dark rust. Even the sheet metal chimney, which flares out as it jumps up in telescoping sections, looks composed and fitting. The entrance area, with its collision of forms, is equally inevitable. 'Disharmonious harmony' is here rendered classical and eternal, as if the L.A. School were born under a Mediterranean sky.

What happens next to en-formality, having reached this degree of self-conscious understanding, is anyone's guess. The danger, as with all authentic and successful styles, is inflation and debasement. Probably it will continue as both a creative tradition and ersatz, like the Japanese Wabi and Sabi styles, an approach with its high and low versions. As a way of dealing with the informal heterogeneity of Los Angeles it is too relevant to be dropped and, as it continues to spread throughout the world, others will take up its peculiar virtues, for it is particularly adept at signifying otherness.

*RIGHT: Propaganda Films, 1988, axonometric; OPPOSITE FROM ABOVE LEFT TO RIGHT: Tisch-Avnet, entrance tower, Los Angeles, 1991 (Tom Bonner); Goldberg/Green House, entry canopy – plan/section/elevation; Goldberg/Green House, rear view (Tom Bonner); Virgin Records, Beverly Hills, floor plan, 1992; Propaganda Films, Los Angeles, 1988 (Tom Bonner); Virgin Records, 1992.*

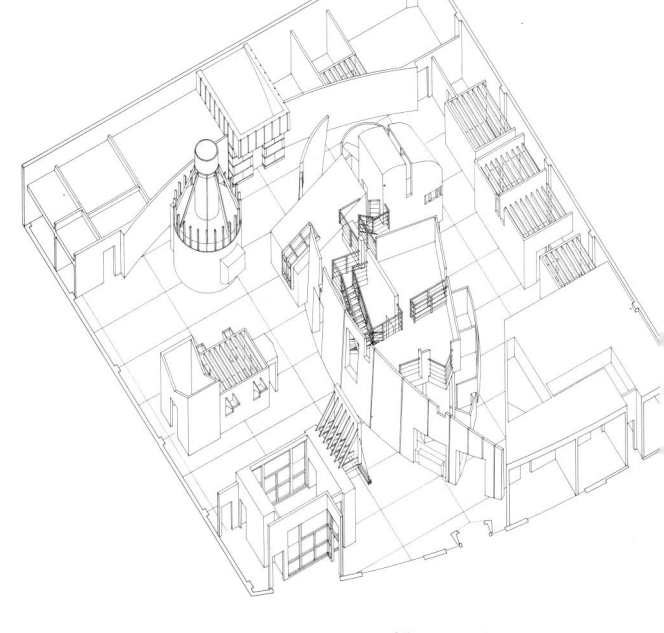

*(44, 45) Frank Israel, Bright and Associates: the gentle juxtapositions of a village turned in on itself.*

*OPPOSITE: (45a) Frank Israel, Bright and Associates, warehouse conversion, Venice, 1988-90. The axonometric shows the sequence of heteromorphic spaces: leaning cube, perspectival tunnel, semi-cone, triangle, arched offices, curved piazza and open space.*

## BACK TO WORK – THE 1990s

Aside from en-formality the L.A. School has made one other contribution to the architectural world, which has also been taken up in other cities: the workplace as urban village. This often amounts to an office as a small city turned inside-out. Post-modern architects in other cities have contributed to this new paradigm. There is the neo-expressionist NMB bank in Amsterdam, the hanging gardens of the Landeszentral bank in Frankfurt, and Hiroshi Hara's office village in Tokyo, but these are all new buildings on a bulldozed site. The Los Angeles architects – Frank Israel, Morphosis, Eric Owen Moss and Gehry – have developed instead the art of converting large warehouses into internalized streets and squares. Part of the reason is pragmatic: these externally disguised, informal types turn their back on the real, hostile street for security reasons, and they retrofit an old structure because it is cheap.

They are like a geode with a rough, weather beaten facade and a *luxe* interior, but the luxury is something else. The stained concrete is polished just so, the sheet metal is carefully chosen to be both aggressive like the real street and artfully twisted and over-detailed with a thousand bolts and unnecessary structural members which say 'this is the real craftsmanship of a post-industrial society, not the Disneyland version'. The message? The raw and uncooked are more nutritious than the pseudo-reality of CityWalk.

The art of en-formality is a high art for office work, in many ways much more suitable than the totally new building. An office, where most of the labor force in the First World will spend most of its time, must be more than a one-dimensional factory for work – much more. It must incorporate other building types – the home and place of relaxed entertainment. This is especially true during the electronic revolution where many people find it more attractive and functional to telecommute. Already Los Angeles has more office-at-home space than other cities. Whereas most metropolitan areas have twenty square feet of office space per person – New York has twenty-eight – the electronic cottages of L.A. have reduced in-town office space to fifteen.[26] The place of work must become ambiguous, domestic and heterogeneous to survive.

Frank Israel has converted several warehouses into offices and understands the genre as much as his fast moving clients – advertizing agencies, design companies, film and record businesses – all typical of the post-industrial labor force. I find his transformation of the old Eames Studio the most successful, because the interaction between the present and past, figure and ground, is most balanced. One approaches this former warehouse, and modernist studio, by way of two tough billboards – one of grey sheet metal, the other a triangle of glass brought to a very aggressive point where you enter. After these and other acknowledgements of a hostile environment, one enters a tiny village turned inside-out. The arrival space is a yellow stucco tower open to the sky, with jutting balconies of – what else? – grey sheet metal (44). From this inverted Italian campanile one is shunted through a dark sheet metal tunnel, to arrive at the third building within a building – the conference room in the shape of an inverted cone (45). To the right one finds the main avenue of the village, with private streets and offices, placed under the grid of the exposed trusses. As in all these conversions metal gusset-plates, wooden beams and hanging duct-work are polished up to become essential icons of work and regular markers of space. Further on the avenue widens slightly to form a curved piazza and then the space constricts before opening out to end in a large open area.[27]

The plan reveals all the conventions of post-modern space that have been current since Venturi and Moore developed the tradition in

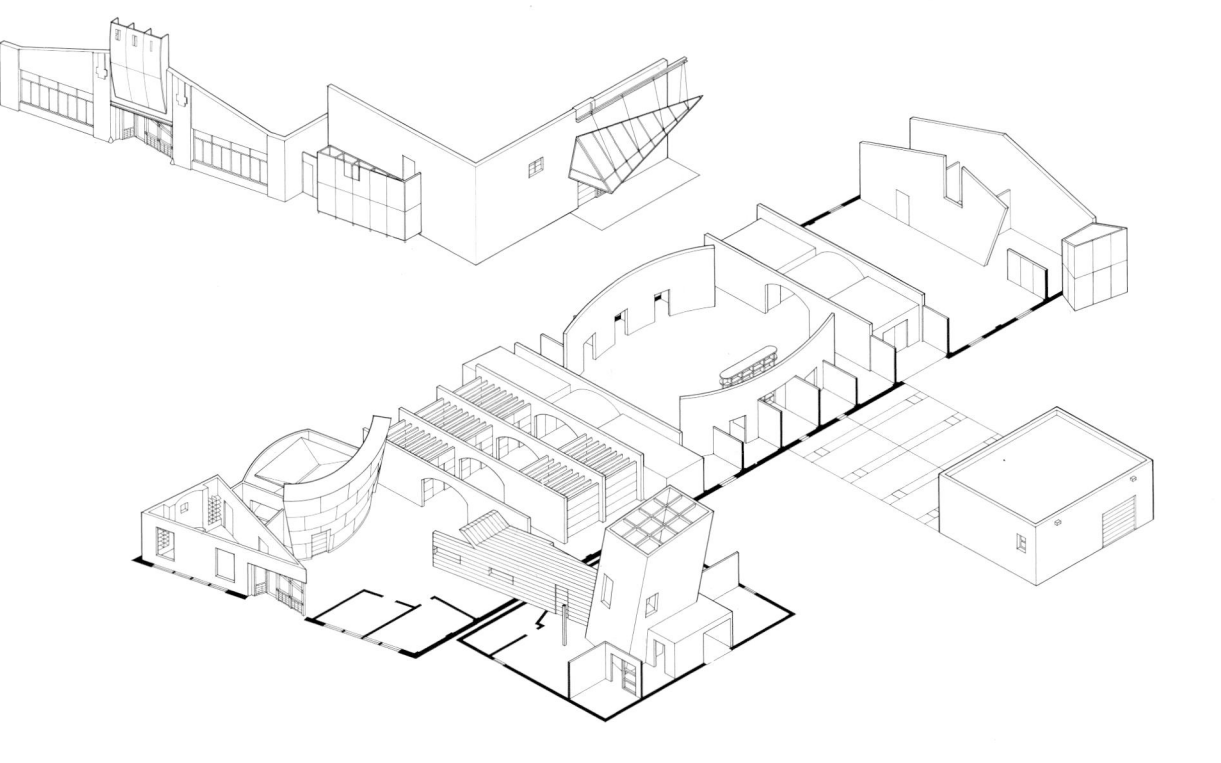

the sixties: the juxtaposition of skewed and distorted figures, positive and negative reversals, ambiguity, collage and paradox. But it is done with a sensibility that is particular to L.A. and Israel.

Among the many workplace conversions that have created the distinctive L.A. type, two stand out as supreme examples of the ad hoc art. One is by Eric Owen Moss, a quintessential Los Angeles character. A sometime weight-lifter who looks like Barry Manilow crossed with an intellectual, Moss accentuates certain aspects of the straight-forward and idiosyncratic, perfect character traits for converting dumb-warehouses into sensual enigmas. A didactic strain runs through his work. Like James Stirling he cuts up and explodes parts of his buildings to show what they are made of, knowing this appeals to the mind, but it also comes from his teaching at Sci Arc. He calls this didactic exposure 'the railroad car theory' of beauty: the idea that 'the erogenous quality of machinery', most evident in railroad cars, can be conveyed when buildings are 'dissected' and 'understood rationally . . . in a scientific sense'.[28] But it is not the perfectly working machine aesthetic of Modernism he is interested in:

> The railroad car in this discussion has grease on the wheels, and sometimes goes off the tracks. It's like the helicopters Jimmy Carter sent to Iran that didn't work because they got sand caught in the propellers. It's that kind of machine.[29]

Grease in the wheels, exposed gears, wires, chains and garage doors that sport their clunky mechanisms comprise a series of fetishistic images that every now and then slip into the rubber and chain cult. Moss has been crowned by Philip Johnson, and in his own monograph no less, the 'Jeweler of Junk'.

Johnson sees him in an alternative tradition of Arts and Craft modernists from Sullivan to Scarpa and, while this has some truth, it carefully overlooks the much more obvious, local line: from the Newsoms to the Greene and Greene plumbing fixtures as architecture, from the machine adhocism of Eames and Schindler to the chain-link and sheet metal of Gehry – that is the real pedigree. It makes Moss the ultimate L.A. designer, a true 'critical regionalist'. He excavates pre-existing structures in order to cut out and accentuate their qualities, he orients to the freeways and other local points he can find, and he elevates the L.A. funk aesthetic to an ugly/beautiful level.

Some of his work is over-labored and self-indulgent, but the modestly titled '8522 National Boulevard' in Culver City is a masterpiece. It is the conversion of five light 1920s industrial warehouses into the near perfect 'office' environment. The plan reveals once again the office-village with its central street – in the shape of an L – and two public 'piazzas' and four semi-public spaces, conference rooms or juncture points, within the separate office areas (46, 47).

The ratio of figure to ground, public to private, monument to urban fabric, is about one to five, a ratio of the historic city, like Rome, and one which gives the key points proper emphasis. Furthermore they occur here quite naturally at the beginning, middle and end of the L-route. This street is handled in a somewhat anonymous manner as a white background subtly lit from above so the rafters glow with a complex, bouncing light. The old warehouse trusses are interlaced with new ones, and this deft weaving extends to the office walls each side, which are layered as independent arches, pier and window-wall (46). Hence the layering works as a set of discrete scenes which allow glimpsed views in and out of the office, rather the way a traditional Japanese street or Arab casbah provides these veiled, in-between spaces. It also appears, like Israel's office villages, as the urban landscape turned inside-out and built as a series of stage-sets.

Hollywood is never far away from the L.A. School, but the mood could not be further from 'Have a Nice Day'. Actually some of the arts and design groups that inhabit this tiny village might work for Hollywood, and Moss and his developer Frederick Smith are quite consciously trying to cut across boundaries of taste and ideology.

(46) Eric Owen Moss, 8522 National Boulevard, Culver City, 1989-91. The L-shaped 'street' starts at an outdoor ellipse, turns at a fragmented ellipse and culminates at a truncated elliptical conference room. The grid of labyrinthine office space forms a layered background.

> The definition of an intelligible building – the kind into which accountants, lawyers and film makers can go – is changing. You can put on a Brooks Brothers suit and go into 8522 National Boulevard and sell your stuff and be totally comfortable. (You don't have to be the hippest guy on the street.) The owners of such projects will exploit that; it allows them to move into areas that are a little less costly . . . [Frederick Smith] is ready to let his conception – or the architect's conception – direct the selling, as opposed to letting the selling direct the architecture . . . He's very unusual in that he takes the consequences of the risk.[30]

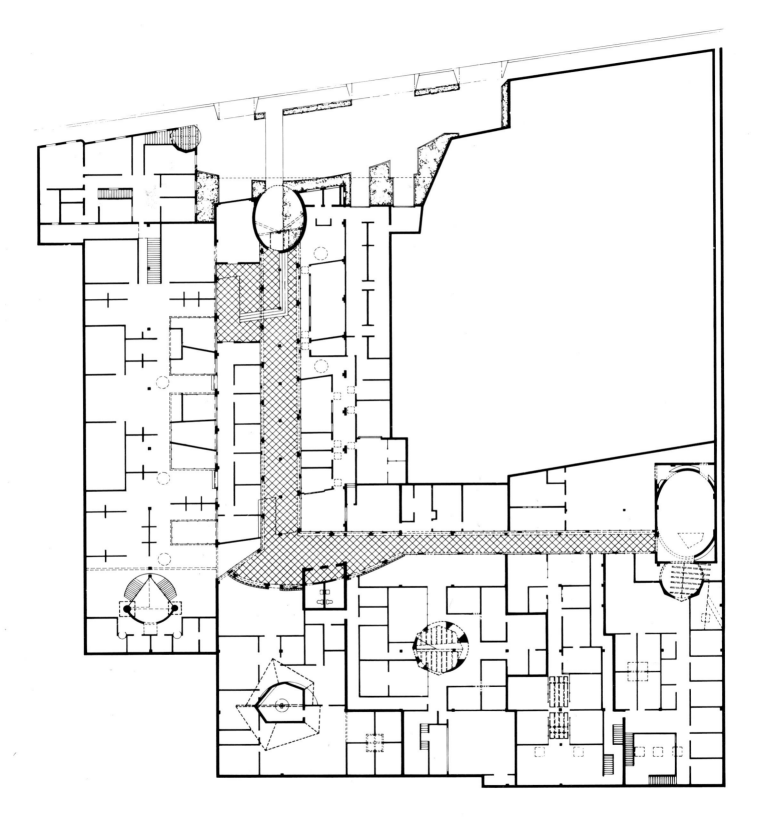

In such descriptions Moss conveys what is evident in his work: the intention to be both ordinary and idiosyncratic, further contradictions that constitute en-formality.

There are two places where 8522 culminates in semi-public space worthy of the name. One is what Moss calls a 'street corner' and 'cross axis', an office intersection which is like a carved out solid of blue-green cheese (47). The thick walls leave heavy voids, or protrude into the room as triangular slices, but their enigmatic quality comes from the way they contrast with the truss and pier which crashes through them, and the fact that they result from a very odd overlapping of circular and octagonal geometries which also interpenetrate. Thus when you arrive at this 'piazza' carved out of urban fabric, it is uncannily both fresh and familiar at the same time.

The other monumental space is equally enigmatic, and even more successful at mixing heterogeneous codes, for in this conference room an elliptical cone of plywood provides a very pleasing enclosure while parts of the old building – a brick wall, pier, window and skylight – are allowed to break into this figure (49). The effect of these interlocking codes really is magical, even disorientating in a convivial sort of way. It is perhaps better not to understand how the trick is done, but it has something to do with tilting a regular shape – the elliptical cone – with dimensions that are both bigger than the original floor and smaller than the roof. Such spaces, and their colliding skylights, penetrate what is in effect an informal but intricate urban tissue. The language cuts across categories, tastes and time frames in a way that is canonic to post-modern literature – that of Umberto Eco, John Barth and Salman Rushdie – and it is no surprise that Moss is an admirer of James Joyce.[31] For Joyce's Dublin we have Moss' Culver City, a near perfect reflection of this area's heterogeneity caused by transitory activity, the mirror image of the fast-changing 'multiclave'.

Just as heteroglot in its nature is Main Street, Venice, where Frank Gehry has designed another converted office-village, which is, along with 8522, an exemplar of the new genre. This one consists of an older warehouse conversion at the back, and a new set of buildings in front, for the advertizing agency Chiat/Day/Mojo.

The context is as mixed as it can be: Main Street commerce and up-market restaurants hit beach bums and dossers' pads hidden in the bushes – looking straight at the executive conference room of Chiat, right into the binoculars (48).

*(47) Eric Owen Moss, plan of 8522. The street corner/cross-axis, one of the semi-public monumental spaces with the old structure breaking through and a collision of skylights.*

*OPPOSITE AND PAGE 72: (46a & 47a) Eric Owen Moss, plans and drawings of 8522 showing the spaces and structures carved into and out of each other – insertions which are reminiscent of Charles Moore's work, but which have a much greater toughness and sense of melancholic angst.*

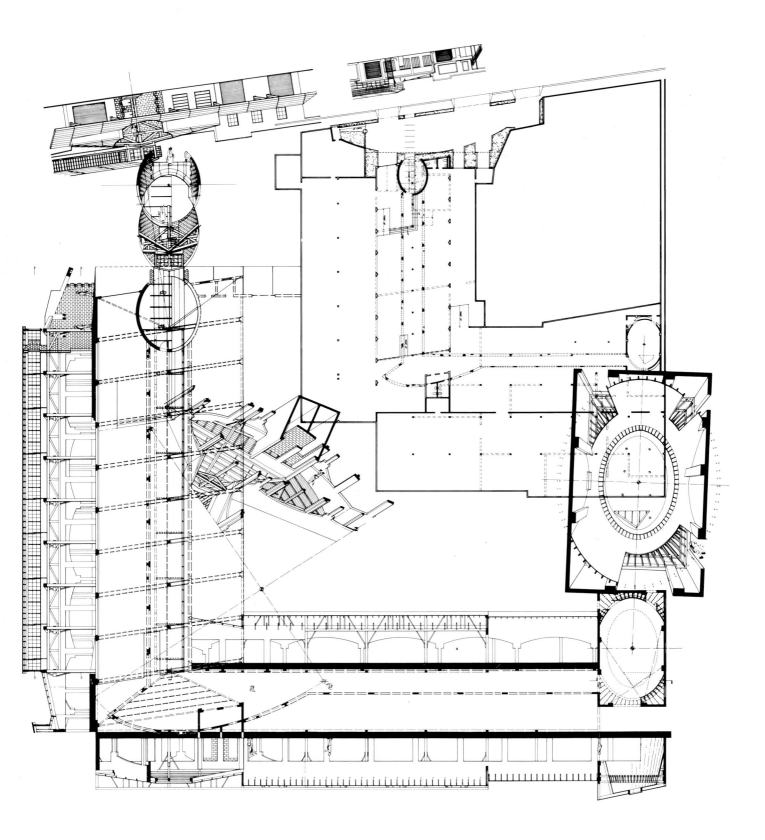

*(48) Venice context with Jonathan Borofsky's* Clown

*PAGE 73: (49) Eric Owen Moss, 8522. The elliptical conference room with its tilted cone and frieze of studs in counterpoint with the existing brickwork and piers – the dialogue of different periods and tastes.*

Across the street to one side is a classical Corinthian arcade brought to a full stop by the gigantic figure of Jonathan Borofsky's *Hermaphroditic Clown*, (its unofficial title), a running man-woman with ballerina legs and a mustache, while to the other sides are dumb stucco boxes, ding-bat apartments and the usual assortment of sheds and warehouses. To a certain extent Gehry's collection of small-scale fragments summarizes the spirit of the place, mixing ordinary, anonymous boxes with slightly veiled images – a white boat or fish to the left – and copper trees and tree trunks to the right. The metaphors are understated, ambiguous and somewhat appropriate, both to the context, near the ocean, and the function (the tree branches serve as sun screens). Even the most explicit image, the binoculars designed by Claes Oldenburg and Coosje van Bruggen serve appropriate functions, as a triumphal archway to the parking lot, and a very sardonic emblem for an ad agency.

But its relevance consists in the small-block planning and office-village layout. As the plan shows, we again have the satisfying ratio of foreground to background, image to abstraction, of about one to five (51a). Like a Renaissance palazzo the front is for show, the back to fill out the lot and form positive left-over space. There is the customary mixture of informal and regular layout which we have come to expect: the work stations organized on a grid, the conference rooms placed in a more free-form shape and surface cores or piazzas punctuating the fabric. In the refurbished warehouse at the back a relaxed urbanity prevails, created by a grid of major avenues, minor streets and monuments set into the fabric.

Here the sting is taken out of the modern office slab with its typical open-planning and utilitarian regimentation. *Bürolandschaften*, office landscaping meant to increase security and control of the work force, is asserted and subverted at the same time: the work stations are open to view, but partially veiled behind screens of studs which form the streets (51). Another factor mediating the central control is the crossing of categories. Because it is an ad agency where the owners collect art, and display some of the products they have featured, one walks through a strange forest of symbols and signs. A real car is on the 'street' (does the Mini work, or is it a present?); a basketball net is next to a sculpture and painting (is it for playing or looking at?). One conference room is a Gehry fish (or is it merely a conveniently curved room formed by the cheapest of L.A. techniques, the exposed stud wall?). The multiple meanings are clearly intended to represent the different voices that make up the city.

Finally, in one part of the office-village is a place set apart from the noise and bustle of the city and workplace – an inner sanctum, something akin to a sacred or contemplative space, a room constructed of cardboard and corrugated paper. This is another magical place, as original and peaceful as those of Eric Owen Moss, but one inflected more towards silence and thought: it cuts down the sound and reverberation to nothing (52, 53). It is like being in an anechoic chamber, so silent you can hear your heart beat. With its interior *oculus* allowing a shaft of California light to move through the conical dome, it is reminiscent of other sacred spaces, such as the Pantheon in Rome. The comparison may sound far-fetched, but the idea is not so absurd as it appears, for why shouldn't a large office – the equivalent of a village – have one area given over to silence and contemplation?

The main point of hetero-architecture is to accept the different voices that create a city, suppress none of them, and make from their interaction some kind of greater dialogue. The Russian critic Mikhail Bakhtin, who formulated the idea of heteroglossia and dialogic, shows their possibilities for creativity.[32] Dialogic underlines the double nature of words that always entail two different attitudes at the same time: that of the speaker and that of the listener about to become a speaker. The dialogue is thus equally determined by at least two different codes, by words shared by addresser and addressee. And if this is true, then it is fundamentally open and oriented towards a future world, for no one can determine the outcome of a true dialogue, which might go in any direction.

Gehry and the L.A. School, particularly in these warehouse conversions for the workplace, combine many texts, many voices. Dialogues between the formal and informal, the present and the past, the industrial and vernacular, violence and safety, and the animal and the mechanical. There is even an understated, half suppressed, dialogue between the utilitarian and the spiritual: Israel, Moss and Gehry, time and again, take a conference room, put it in a formal shape, juxtapose it with exposed beams and mechanical ducts, and then give it an ethereal skylight that turns it into a small chapel.

The opposite of hetero-architecture is not homo- but mono-architecture; that is, building which is reduced, exclusive, over-integrated, perfected and sealed off from life and change. Mies van der Rohe's architecture, minimalism, most classicisms, most

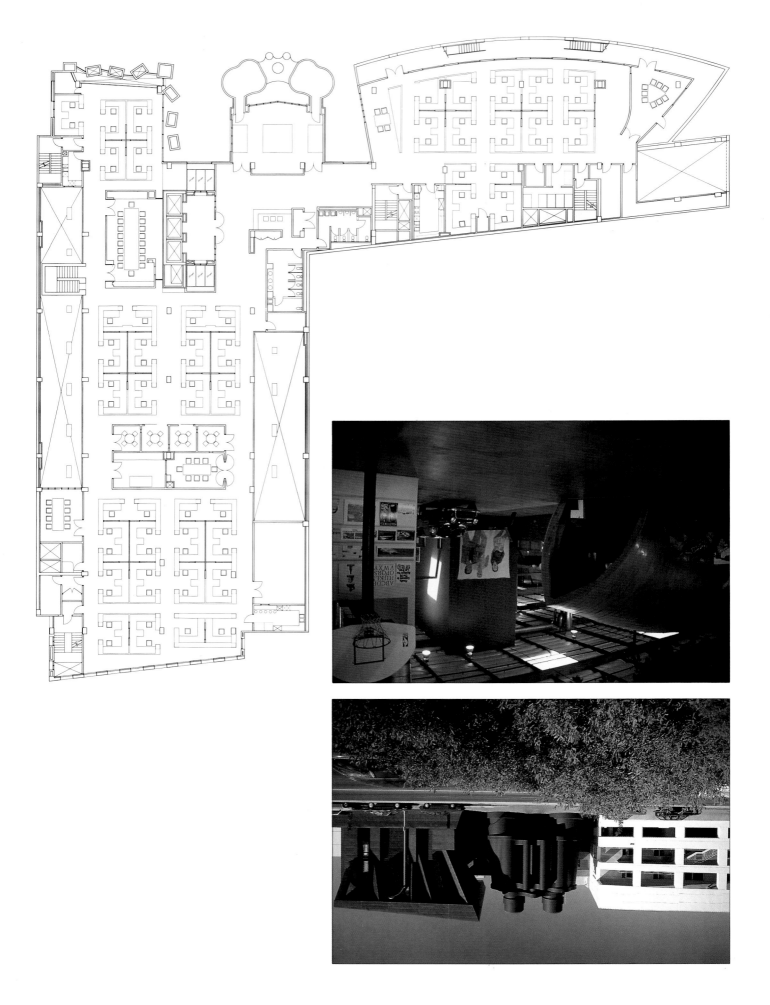

corporate and academic building – that is, most professional architecture – is monological and limited by definition and legal contract. After the drawings are made, the bids are sealed, the specifications are written, it is a deterministic affair. Any nagging ambiguities and changes are to be disputed in court. With the L.A. School, particularly Gehry and Moss, it is often not clear when, or even if, the building is ever finished. How can you sue an architect when the building makes a virtue of accidents, mistakes and improvisations?

It is this improvisational, heteroglottic nature which is so characteristic of Los Angeles as a whole and the L.A. Style in particular, a mode which, because of the information world and similar conditions, can be found in several cities around the globe. Just as the office-village has become a prototype to be shared, so perhaps will the peculiar Los Angeles workplace, with its mixture of categories, functions and voices. If America must reinvent more adequate attitudes to work in the nineties, and re-establish a public realm, then convivial models can be found here.

Nevertheless, architecture, even when pluralistic, is never enough. It is no answer to the lack of effective political pluralism, which can be created only by civic institutions, prevailing customs and concerted willpower. Architecture can accomplish much by accepting and celebrating heterogeneity, but it is no substitute for a better politics, economic opportunities and community cohesion. This is quite obvious in the high crime rate, the conflict between ethnic groups and classes, and the prevailing fear indicated by the prevalence of security devices. Fortress architecture is one response to dismal economic realities and a lack of political pluralism, and the events of 1992 that really shook the city and the other: a small earthquake followed by five days of riots.

*OPPOSITE ABOVE: (50) Frank Gehry, Chiat/Day/Mojo Office, Venice, design 1985, realization 1989-91. White boat (fish?), binoculars and copper trees – images for Main Street and the Pacific Rim – placed in front of a small anonymous block.*

*OPPOSITE CENTER: (51) Frank Gehry, Chiat/Day/Mojo interior of converted warehouse. Interweaving of categories, urban types, new incisions and old warehouse.*

*OPPOSITE BELOW: (51a) Frank Gehry, Chiat/Day/Mojo, plans, 1989. Streets, avenues, grids set off against monumental piazzas.*

*ABOVE: (52, 53) Frank Gehry, Chiat/Day/Mojo Conference Room. A sacred space that sucks up the sound, a space set apart.*

# CHAPTER FOUR

# WHAT CAUSED THE JUSTICE RIOTS?

On April 29th 1992 just after 3.00pm, four police officers were acquitted of beating a black Los Angeles motorist named Rodney King. The verdict was a shock to most people, even if it was delivered from a white-dominated courtroom far from the city, because the beating was so clearly sadistic and unfair, and seen to be so. For more than a year much of America had watched it on TV, since an amateur video-enthusiast happened to film it. There was no doubt that King had been beaten when he was down and not a threat: kicked, pummeled and prodded with a Taser stun gun while a dozen or so police extras watched the four go to work.

At 3.43pm on the 29th a young black store clerk hurled a rock at a passing white motorist. Contrary to stereotype, his spontaneous act of fury did not occur in the poorest part of L.A., but in Hyde Park, a district which is relatively solvent – its unemployment rate lower than Venice's, its level of home ownership higher than Pasadena's.[33] Soon thereafter, at 4.17pm, violence erupted to the east at the intersection of Florence and Normandie Avenues – an area that became known as the symbolic center of the riots – where this time a white truck driver, Reginald Denny, was filmed live being pulled from his truck and beaten almost to death – a video once again shown repeatedly to America on TV.

The broadcast of this event late that afternoon had an immediate effect on the South Central part of Los Angeles, magnifying social unrest until it spread to become 'the most violent American civil disturbance since the Irish poor burned Manhattan in 1863'.[34] Television and other electronic media amplified the message and brought out the public as they had done in Eastern Europe in 1989. 'Image looters', those looking for adventure, and gang members of the feared Crips and Bloods who had been fighting each other for years, saw and heard the message and quickly joined the frey.

This much the world watched as it was rebroadcast by CNN and the BBC around the globe. What the media missed, however, was an understanding of the deeper motives for rebellion and how the insurrection spread. A demographic map makes this clear. The

*OPPOSITE: (54) South Central L.A., the second day of the riots. (Robert Lerner)*

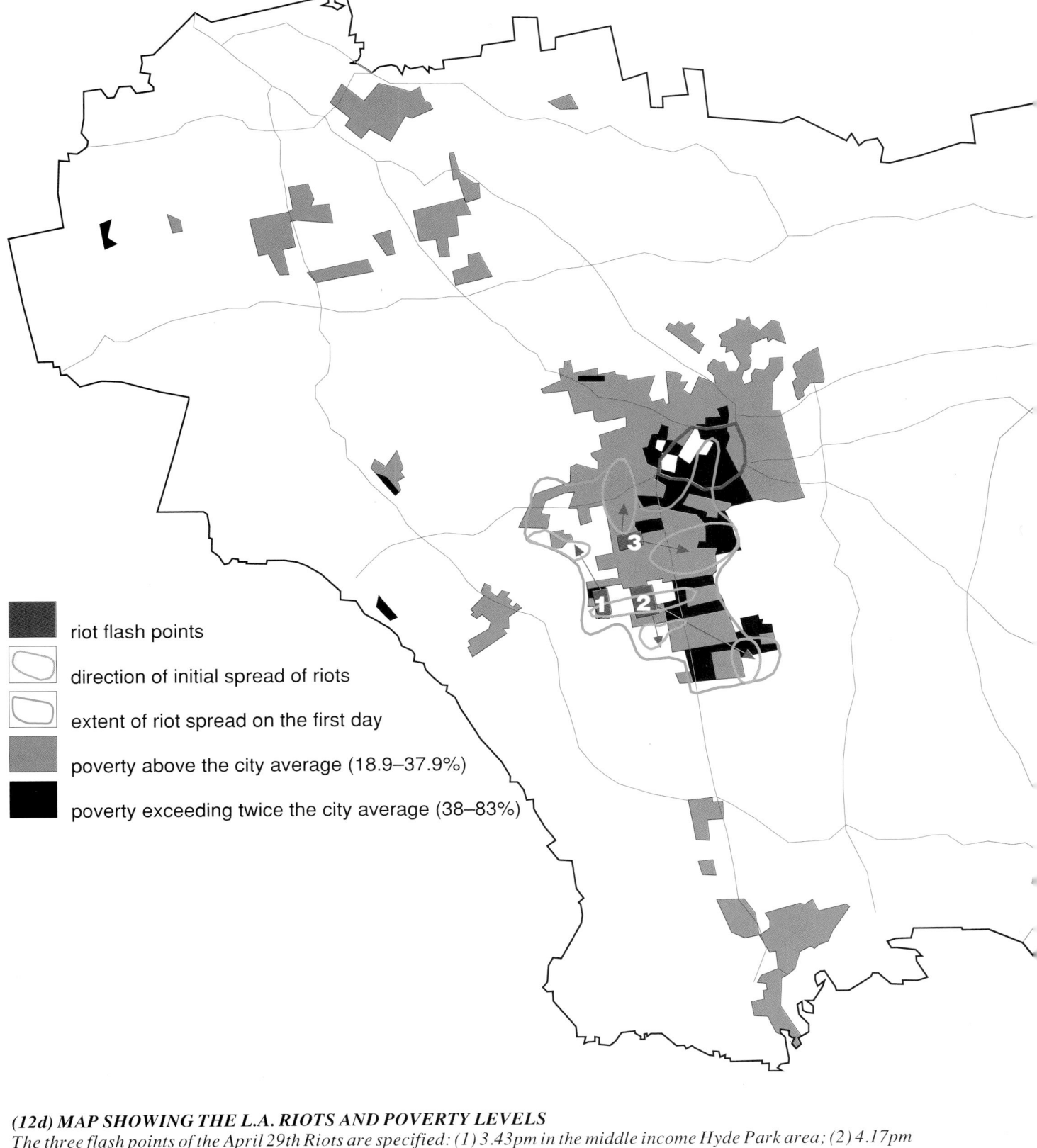

| | |
|---|---|
| | riot flash points |
| | direction of initial spread of riots |
| | extent of riot spread on the first day |
| | poverty above the city average (18.9–37.9%) |
| | poverty exceeding twice the city average (38–83%) |

**(12d) MAP SHOWING THE L.A. RIOTS AND POVERTY LEVELS**

*The three flash points of the April 29th Riots are specified: (1) 3.43pm in the middle income Hyde Park area; (2) 4.17pm at the intersection of Florence and Normandie; (3) 4.21pm at the intersection of Normandie and Martin Luther King. Also indicated are the areas to which the riots spread or where they erupted spontaneously between 3.43 and 10.00 pm (data based on the number of police phone calls).*

*The five-day riot encompassed a larger territory and focused on Koreatown, where most of the retail shops were destroyed. (See detail map on pages 82-83 to see the correlation between areas of poverty, ethnic grouping and the riots).*

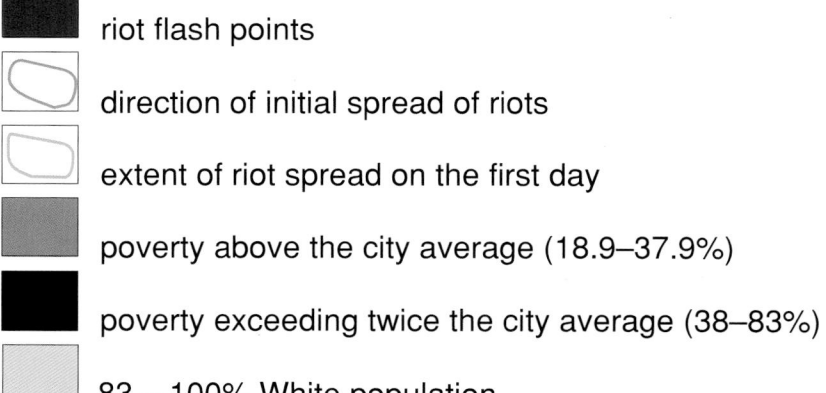

| | |
|---|---|
| ⬛ | riot flash points |
| ⬭ | direction of initial spread of riots |
| ⬭ | extent of riot spread on the first day |
| ◻ | poverty above the city average (18.9–37.9%) |
| ⬛ | poverty exceeding twice the city average (38–83%) |
| ◻ | 83 – 100% White population |
| ⬛ | 59.8 – 93.4% Black population |
| ◻ | 50.1 – 75.6% Asian population |
| ◻ | 50.1 – 98.6% Hispanic population |

**DETAIL OF OVERLAY SHOWING THE ETHNIC, POVERTY AND RIOT MAPS OF L.A.**
*This shows that most of the strife was inter-ethnic and located between concentrations of black, Hispanic and Korean populations, a supposition born out by the number of arrests. This suggests that while the immediate cause was the unjust decision in the Rodney King case, the riot was fueled by the lethal mixture of ethnic and economic competition at the bottom of the ladder.*

uprising started in the more middle-class areas of the black community where the *enragés* felt their stake in society was threatened. Akin to the classical revolutions – America 1776, France 1789 – it was not the poor who started things, but the conscientious and ambitious. The latter, suddenly finding they had been let down by an unfair judiciary and police state, immediately concluded that to continue in hard work would be pointless.

'If you're a hardworking person who spends eight, ten, twelve hours a day working and saving', said Troy Duster, head of the UC Berkeley Institute for Social Change, 'you can imagine the fury if something in the system were to reveal that it was all really corrupt'.[35] This assessment was echoed by many residents of the moderately well-off neighborhoods where the riots started: 'This has nothing to do with money', said Barbara Knox from Florence and Normandie. 'It's about being treated with dignity'. 'We eat, we sleep, we have clothes, we don't want for anything except being treated fairly', said another from the same area – 'To some, you're still just a nigger.'

The gathering storm of outrage moved both to the poorer Hispanic and richer Korean areas. In five days of rioting fifty people were killed, over a billion dollars of property was destroyed, seventeen thousand people were arrested and five thousand ended up in court. Contrary to conventional opinion, this was not simply the senseless riot of a black underclass. It was something more complex and dynamic, perhaps a new archetype for the twenty-first century: the first multi-ethnic uprising, the first civil disturbances led by several minorities trapped in inner city poverty. As the Rand Corporation pointed out, fifty-one per cent of the defendants in court were Hispanic, only thirty-six per cent black and the rest divided among the other L.A. minorities.[36]

Minoritization, the typical post-modern phenomenon where most of the population forms the 'other', where most city dwellers feel distanced from the power structure, put on its first psychodrama and display of collective alienation. Part of this was motivated by greed and opportunism, and the psychic distance provided by a TV spectacle where others could be seen looting from burning shops as if they belonged to no one. 'Why not me too?' was the underlying assumption of the 'image looters'. Sixty-eight per cent of the damaged buildings were retail stores, the next highest figure – a mere six per cent – were restaurants, making this look like the first consumerist conflagration in history.[37]

But if the spread of the riots had mixed motives – greed, alienation, boredom – its deep cause was the sense of frustration among the blacks. As sociologists have shown with regard to L.A., simply being black reduces one's wages by thirty-five per cent, a figure that has risen since 1969 from thirty per cent.[38] Thus, endemic black poverty was one motive. The rioters' vengeance, according to Mike Davis, the writer who knows more about 'real' L.A. than anyone else, was aimed at Koreatown. There ninety per cent of the Korean-owned liquor stores, markets and 'swap meets' were wiped out.[39] Why should this minority take the brunt? Not only because the Koreans were newly arrived immigrants, not only because they had become successful middle entrepreneurs displacing blacks from neighborhoods and jobs, but because of one act that represented the widespread legal injustice blacks had been suffering – the recent shooting of the fifteen-year-old Latasha Harlins. Her fate, even more than the televised beating of Rodney King, was the ultimate symbol of inequity. Shot in the back of the head by a Korean grocer after a dispute over a bottle of orange juice, her assassin was let off with a five hundred dollar fine and some community service, a clear indication that taking a black child's life is regarded as less significant than tax evasion. Hence, when Rodney King's verdict was announced the black community, and the Crips and Blood gangs, were already poised to strike against society in general and the Koreans in particular.

Nevertheless, this was a multi-ethnic riot reflecting almost exactly the demographic make-up of South Central L.A. which is sixty per cent Hispanic and thirty-five per cent black, figures which we have seen are nearly the same as the percentage of arrests. In analyzing the deeper causes of unrest several surveys have focused on the increasing poverty of the Hispanic population in the 1980s showing that this group constitutes 58 per cent of the poor – by far the majority, as compared with 20.5 per cent made up of non-Hispanic white and 13.4 per cent who are black.[40] People often overlook the poor white sector, just as they often overlook the large manufacturing base of the city because, according to stereotype neither are supposed to exist.

Another underlying cause was the uncontrolled growth of the city; the influx of people from Mexico and other Third World countries. Seven hundred and fifty thousand immigrants have come since 1980 – many of them illegally – and these optimistic adventurers in search of the good life, like the millions before them, found that opportunities

– at the bottom of the ladder – were disappearing as fast as they arrived.[41] Whereas the California-American Dream was still a reality at the top, the recession hit the poor first, and in any case during the 1980s the gap between the rich and the poor was becoming a chasm.

The 1990 census showed that forty per cent of city residents were foreign-born, an increase of two-thirds in ten years. When a city has that many new arrivals speaking different languages – and the economy turns down – it is not surprising if the result is ethnic strife. In the past this has been overtly racist, such as black-versus-white in the Watts uprising of 1965. However, in the future, with Hispanic and Asian people making up well over fifty per cent of the population, the polarizations are likely to be more complex and dynamic, like the shifting power struggles in the former Soviet Union and Yugoslavia.

One might compare Los Angeles with these two multi-ethnic conglomerates – no longer nation-states. Its economy is much more dynamic and its population more rich at a micro-scale in ethnic diversity, while it is much smaller in size. Its various ethnic groups and lifestyle clusters are spread out in much smaller units comprising a dazzling kaleidoscope rather than a more clear cut pattern of separated groups. Think of it as a painting by Seurat rather than a Mondrian, or an abstract mosaic with all-over patterns rather than a map of Europe with clear boundaries. The fine kaleidescopic grain means that large-scale social movements catalyzing the whole city are unlikely, and while L.A. has some concentrations, like Watts, where the population is over ninety per cent black, these homogeneities are small in size compared to the blocks of Muslims, Croatians, Serbians and Bosnians in the former Yugoslavia.

According to one reading, the African-Americans are at constant war with a society that is suppressing them and the Justice Riot is merely the visible expression of this continuing battle – in effect a class war transformed into an ethnic struggle against the Koreans who have usurped most of the jobs and stores. The strife is continual. In August 1992 a new county record of two hundred and sixty-three homicides was reached, two-thirds by gunshot; more than those killed that month in Yugoslavia.[42] A truce was called for a 'no-killing' Labor Day weekend and, like the cease-fire between the Crips and Bloods after the riot, it was largely successful.

Conceiving Los Angeles as a tiny Europe of thirty-eight nations, or a fractious Yugoslavia, is heuristically helpful as it throws into sharp relief an overlooked truth: the city's problems are pre-eminently

*OPPOSITE: (55, 56) Burning mini-malls, the revenge against consumerism and small shop owners.*

*(57) Real-Riot-Realism. (Robert Lerner)*

global and they will not be solved if they are treated as local or urban problems alone. If L.A. is the most minoritized city in the world, then it should also be conceived both as one of the smaller nations and as a harbinger of other world cities to come. Perhaps we should think of ethnic battle in Los Angeles as periodic if not chronic. It is not as deeply rooted as in Jerusalem with its four thousand years of religious, tribal warfare. There are no explicit ideological differences between the Koreans, blacks, Hispanics, Anglos and others; many of them are Christian, particularly the Koreans, and they all subscribe, in varying degrees, to the California-American Dream – even if some are excluded from it. Americans at large refuse to admit that the melting-pot cannot work, that every group – if they continue to work hard enough and expand – cannot find its piece of the expanding economic pie.

But with the recession, the competition for low-paying jobs and mass immigration – much of it illegal – the struggle is likely to continue. The environment is likely to become more defensive, walled off and inward-looking; ubiquitous signs protecting private property – 'full armed response' – will probably get nastier.

Two dim hopes are on the horizon. One is the 'Rebuild L.A.' program instituted by Mayor Tom Bradley, wherein five hundred companies are set to invest one billion dollars in two years, while the Federal government has allotted $l.35 billion worth of loans and grants.[43] The problem with this, six months on from the riots in November 1992, is that most of the money is going into the National Guard, state police and debris removal, while relatively little is ending up with the families who need it.

Pluralism and the unofficial economy, which are benefits to the city in times of expansion, are now working against recovery. Bureaucrats and ad hoc groups are contesting the programs and jockeying for power. Peter Uberroth, the businessman selected by Mayor Bradley to lead Rebuild L.A., expressed the frustrations to his group: 'There have been lots of hearings, a lot of people arguing about territory, but nothing [has] happened'.[44] One reason is that a clear governmental program is not in place. Another is that small entrepreneurs among the immigrant groups are not used to complying with government requirements, even paying taxes. Thus fifty-five per cent of the applications for loans and grants have been turned down as inadequate or fraudulent – an incredibly high percentage. Perhaps *something* will come of Federal promises and Rebuild L.A., but whatever that something is, it will favor economic interests outside the South Central area.

This explains the second dim hope for the future, put forward by the L.A. branch of the California Green Party and such a black national leader as Louis Farrakhan, the idea of black economic self-determination, black capitalism and support for local micro-economies.[45] In the sense that the looting and burning was aimed against the Korean stores, most of which were put out of action, this can already be seen as an operative motive. 'After all', an ex-Crip told Mike Davis, 'we didn't burn our community, just *their* stores'.

Such aggressive comment is especially nasty for those whose livelihoods were destroyed, but it does show that the lack of economic self-determination was an underlying cause of the riots and therefore a key issue which has to be addressed in any cure. The L.A. Greens propose a community banking system, support for local ownership and control, the recycling of profits back into the community, 'co-operative zone funding, co-operative food markets and health care facilities'. They point out rightly that 'only policies that promote community self-determination and self-reliance can lead us to a just and sustainable society', a policy with which the Crips, Bloods and emergent black capitalists might all agree.[46] At issue here are two different views of how the economy should work, the dominant corporate model of 'Rebuild L.A.' and the Green Community model of 'Co-operate L.A.' The latter is much more relevant to the situation, which is why it is included here in the appendix. But the question is not whether the policy is right so much as whether it might gain the support of the many different communities that make up South Central Los Angeles. Perhaps – but divisions and differences are so much part of the post-modern condition that this will be hard to achieve.

### THE RESPONSE:
### DEFENSIBLE ARCHITECTURE AND RIOT-REALISM

It is too early to predict the way architects, contractors and home-owners will respond to the riots, but in an important sense they have already pre-empted the violence by many years. By the late 1970s Moore and Gehry were inventing their different versions of a 'cheapskate aesthetic' which could respond to the reality of street life, with dumb stucco walls and chain-link – both turned into ambiguous signs of inventive beauty and 'keep out' (58). By the late

1980s deconstructionism had swept across the schools of architecture and there were many shades of alienation, heavy-metal expressionism and fortress-design to call on, varying from 'dirty realism' and 'post-holocaust design' to 'dead-tech'. Anthony Vidler could even give these trends a two-hundred-year pedigree in *The Architectural Uncanny*, 1992, summarizing the antecedents of urban anomie with the theories of Pater, Heidegger, Lukács, Freud and the more up-to-date Deconstructionism of Lacan, Derrida and Baudrillard.[47] 'Transcendental homelessness', 'rootlessness' and 'spatial estrangement' were the social facts and values to be represented in this architecture which holds the mirror up to reality.

The shift in architectural discourse, previously given to ideal imagery, should not be underrated. Before this shift there had never been an architecture of positive alienation. It is true that just after the First World War a few German Expressionists tried to fashion a new style of building which represented the recent catastrophes and even the wild sexual longings of the poets and painters of the moment, but a Dada architecture never took hold. And the New Brutalism in Britain, 1960-65, which in some respects tried to turn rough urban reality into a new poetics of building, soon became a

*(58) Frank Gehry, Cabrillo Marine Museum, San Pedro, 1979. The context of an asphalt parking lot surrounded by chain-link, an army base and traffic became the pretext for this early example of 'dirty realism' – an architecture that transforms necessity into an art of hard-edge material, defensible space and the 'ephemeral gauze' of chain-link – here used in an expressionist way.*

*genre de vie* for university campuses and concert halls, more the equivalent of designer blue-jeans than real blue overalls worn by the working class. That class did not take to Brutalist housing-estates; to them they symbolized the all too real brutalism of social deprivation. Deconstructivist architects partly continue the Brutalist version of the 'sophisticates' tough' as ivory-tower Derrideans dispensing frenzied cacophony to the masses, *de haut en bas*. Oh the irony of the avant-garde trying to be 'real', meeting head on those mired in reality looking for ideal images!

*(59) Steven Erhlich, Shatto Recreation Center, Los Angeles, 1991-92. A defensive architecture of corrugated metal, brickwork patterns, concrete and steel survived in an area of rioting without even a graffiti attack. (Robert Lerner)*

In any case, by the late 1980s enough representations of alienation had been talked about, designed and built for us to understand, well before the riots, what a riot realism would be. In Los Angeles the Shatto Recreation Center near Downtown was constructed like a World War Two Quonset hut, from highly defensible galvanized steel rolled in the shape of a ground-hugging parabola that would deflect any explosion (59). Front and back windowless walls were protected by a textured brick to defy graffiti, climbing up in fragmented, growing shapes, at once the image of computer-generated fractals and a crumbling ruin. Many architects, from Aldo Rossi to SITE, had proffered strategies for what could be called 'Neo-Ruinism' – varying from the burnt-out, haunted 'house of the dead' to the peeling fractured archaelogical site. These were not pretty ruins, no eight-eenth-century follies in the garden. Rather they were the beginning of a professional shift, the first time architects could look into the dark of division, conflict and decay, and represent some unwelcome truths.

Among those truths facing heterogeneous Los Angeles was the necessity of supplying 'defensible space'. In 1972 Oscar Newman wrote a book of that name, attacking modern architecture for not supplying clearly defined and clearly owned territory. Instead of the abstract green and open space of Le Corbusier and the housing estate, he proposed a more privatized architecture of walls, keep-out signs, security cameras, security men and private property. Many vandalized housing estates in Britain, and 'the projects' in America, were redesigned along these guidelines, thereby effectively reduc-ing crime at these points (though critics said the defensible architec-ture merely pushed crime elsewhere).

By 1985 Frank Gehry was redesigning a library in Hollywood, which had suffered constant vandalism including arson, with twenty-foot walls and grand sliding entrance gates – all of which said 'fortress' to the L.A. writer Mike Davis, who condemned both the

*(60) Brian Murphy, Hopper House, Venice, Ca., 1986. Defensive, minimalist, understated architecture without windows on the street preceded the riots: the anonymous warehouse-style became a form of urban camouflage for the private house. (Robert Lerner)*

building and the trend.[48] 'Stealth houses', he called the genre as a whole, especially those buildings which dissimulated their luxurious interiors with 'proletarian or gangster facades'. Brian Murphy built several houses in Los Angeles which took defensive architecture to an even greater extreme. The Dixon house, which had been broken into five times before Murphy's treatment, exaggerated the exterior as an alienated ruin – with graffiti, walled-up windows, plywood and tar paper used raw – while the inside became a luxurious, skylit house. For ten years the structure has been 'burglar-proof'.[49] His house for Dennis Hopper carries the schizophrenia even further, having a windowless steel wall and white picket fence on the exterior of a warm domestic interior (60). In such doubly-coded buildings Americans face, for the first time since they fought the Native Americans, a contradiction which has a venerable tradition in Europe, going back to Filippo Brunelleschi and Inigo Jones. The latter proposed a sober, understated exterior which would not attract envy but would still allow an interior to 'fly out licentiously'.

With the gap between rich and poor increasing in the 1980s, even more with the cultural gaps between immigrant groups being exacerbated by mass migration, Americans have finally had to confront the conflict built into pluralism. In Los Angeles forty-four per cent of the adult population was born outside the country. In other cities such as Miami the figure reaches a staggering seventy per cent.

For these reasons, and twelve years of divisive Reaganism, the country is undergoing its first real bout of 'wallification'. The great American tradition – counter to so much of the rest of the world – has been the absence of fences between properties. From suburb as open, flowing parkland to the in-town residence as a streetscape of front doors and open porches, the tradition has continued. Contrast this openness and accessibility to the Pompeian house, or the Chinese courtyard residence or the Jerusalem apartment – all archetypes of defense, estrangement, 'keep out' – and the message is clear. In the former the American Dream presumes neighborliness and a tacit understanding of boundaries, while in the latter the older civilization presumes conflict, difference and a contradiction between public and private realms.

As Los Angeles 'comes of age', it has to confront the contradiction inherent in its open-door policy. For one hundred years it has carried forward the American agenda proclaimed in the Statue of Liberty – give us 'your tired, your poor, your huddled masses yearning to breathe free' – and thrived on the policy. One ethnic group after another defined itself in this open space. Many lifestyle clusters, interest groups and ten million individuals came to the city to assert their particularity and difference from the rest.

But at a certain moment this self-definition by difference reaches a fracturing point, and the population defines itself by what it is against. And then the virtues of pluralism become corresponding vices, out-groups to be feared, either an ethnic or pressure group to be stereotyped: Koreans, or gays, Salvadoreans, or feminists, Hispanics, or hippies, Anglos, or policemen, blacks, or politicians, Iranians, or lawyers, Jews, or students, Vietnamese, or Republicans, Chinese, or free-thinkers, and so on. I have purposely alternated some of the vilified out-groups first to show how incommensurable they are, and second to show they may end up including everybody. Each positive category may turn into a negative epithet of paranoia. The fear of multiculturalism is that the upwards mobility of any one group will entail the downwards mobility of another; positive discrimination may mean that qualified whites will loose jobs because of the color of their skin.

If Los Angeles now contains more such group differences than any other city, it will have to learn both greater tolerance *and* greater respect for boundaries. Architecturally it will have to learn the lessons of Gehry's aesthetic and en-formality: how to turn unpleasant necessities such as chain-link fence into amusing and ambiguous signs of welcome/keep out, beauty/defensible space. Semiotically it will have to come to terms with an important social truth: as the Korean immigrant said when asked about his new-found identity, 'I'll always be a hyphenated-American'. Precisely. This expresses a real insight. The fate and possibility of a pluralist culture which celebrates heterogeneity is to turn *everyone* into hyphenated-Americans.

Self-identity is always created in the double movement of similarity/difference, and Koreans, no more than feminists, want to give up their values to assimilate into the broad universalism that is Middle America. The reason that so many foreigners come to settle in the country has a two-fold motive that I have mentioned in the introduction: to become American *and* achieve self-identity. These two motives often pull in opposite directions, and to reach the latter requires a certain protection that the Bill of Rights supports. Defensible architecture, however regrettable as a social tactic, also protects the rights of individuals and threatened groups.

# CHAPTER FIVE

# IS UNITY POSSIBLE?

Traditionally public architecture – churches, courts, city halls and covered walkways – has always claimed to represent values which a culture shares. A unity of aim and expression is presumed in such building, since the public must understand and pay for it. This obvious point needs reviewing, because it inevitably becomes contested in a pluralist society: 'unity for whom?' is the question. Which interest group is being served when a highway or concert hall is built? In more traditional and integrated cultures such a question does not arise because the answer is assumed. Yet even in Britain things are changing. When part of Windsor Castle burned in November 1992, the question of who should pay for the renewal – the Queen or the tax-payer – immediately became a political issue, with most of the public saying 'both'. In Los Angeles, if they conducted such polls for public building, the answer would be even less clear.

The question of architectural legitimacy is different from political legitimacy, because it has a different time-scale and a greater emphasis on such non-democratic values as creativity and beauty. Furthermore, the split between social meaning and artistic relevance may become endemic, as it has in this century, with mediocre architects receiving most public commissions – Washington DC is the prime example – and the best architects receiving private or commercial building tasks. This problematic situation is normal in many American cities, and nowhere more so than in Los Angeles. There, as I have mentioned, the Downtown and the major public buildings – except for the central library by Bertrand Goodhue, and MOCA by Arata Isozaki – have gone to minor architects. Then, in 1988, Frank Gehry won a limited competition to design the Disney Concert Hall, and for the first time in living memory a leading local architect was given the opportunity to design an important public building (61). The question people ask is: 'will the building bring Los Angeles together; will it be accepted and loved by a heterogeneous culture?' Such a question, after the Los Angeles riots, is understandable and valid for any public architecture, especially that which costs $125 million, the majority of which will be paid by city funds.[50]

*OPPOSITE: (61) Frank Gehry, Walt Disney Concert Hall, Los Angeles, original design 1988, model of the third major revision 1992. Enigmatic white limestone forms lean up and billow out, at once like a flower reaching for the light and a cascade of broken crockery symbolizing the drama of music, noise and the clash of contending voices. (Joshua White)*

Consider first, however, the oddity of such a demand. Why ask architects to do more than religion and politics have done – unify a culture, or express heterogeneous *and* universal ideas. After all, nineteenth-century critics such as Matthew Arnold asked art to fulfill this protean role, and it proved inadequate. Why should a new concert hall succeed? Yet, adequate or not, this is the kind of demand put on public architecture, and it is the discourse which legitimizes public building in the first place. Indeed, when Gehry presented his second version of the hall, in October 1991, Leon Whiteson wrote the kind of legitimizing peroration for the all-important *Los Angeles Times* that one would expect of a president about to justify his inauguration platform. I will quote from it at length, because it illustrates the kind of expectations of public architecture that are typical in a young city, especially a heterogeneous one. It shows the kind of unifying gesture expected of the architect:

> Few buildings in the history of Los Angeles are more important to the life of the city than the proposed Walt Disney Concert Hall on Bunker Hill. Disney Hall is important for several reasons. It will crown Bunker Hill and will be a pivotal link in the cultural corridor along Grand Avenue, between the Music Center and the Museum of Contemporary Art . . . a crucial corner where the cultural corridor intersects the city's civic core that runs along 1st Street down to the City Hall. Most of all, Disney Hall will affirm Los Angeles' coming of age as the West Coast's major cultural center.
>
> For such a vital public building we need an architectural masterpiece, and architect Frank Gehry's design is exactly that.
>
> Gehry's Disney Hall is that rare event – an act of architecture that not only serves its purpose but transcends it as a true work of art. Resembling a galleon in full sail, the Disney Hall complex is a cluster of superbly orchestrated eccentric shapes . . . the flowing curves . . . pay homage to the rounded colonnade of the [adjacent Music] Pavilion . . . Mrs Disney is delighted . . . [the model's presentation to the Venice Biennale] represents U.S. architecture to the world . . .
> Continuing the nautical metaphor expressed in Disney

Hall's exterior, the concert hall resembles a giant rectangular wooden boat Gehry once dubbed 'Noah's Ark' . . . '[51]

The reiteration of the word 'cultural' as the leading honorific implies what many people believe today – that art and culture come before religion and politics. The emphasis on Los Angeles' 'coming of age', Gehry's 'true work of art' and the nautical imagery are also key terms of this discourse. They again imply the primacy of culture and are directed at an important L.A. audience, the art and architectural avant-gardes. Reference to Mrs Disney and the Venice Biennale address a different audience, the more conservative-minded constituency; and a long discussion of the acoustic considerations (not quoted here), justifies the building to yet another group, the businessmen, rationalist readers and musicians. Then Whiteson reaches the largest audience, and the big question of the general public. He quotes Gehry:

> Insofar as a concert hall can be populist, I want the design to avoid an air of cultural intimidation . . . The architecture should invite people in off the street. It should prick the curiosity even of those Angelenos who might normally never attend a performance.[52]

The original scheme had a huge glass foyer opening out to embrace the public; as Gehry said: 'a living room for the city . . . creating the kind of public architecture that it is easy to walk into off the street, and in tune with the relaxed sensibility of Los Angeles' (62). Unfortunately, for functional reasons, this accessible space had to be shrunk back into the limestone 'sails', but the openness of the billowing shapes and the surrounding gardens will still provide accessibility and a welcoming image.

Whiteson ends on the way Gehry 'has finally been embraced by the mainstream cultural establishment in his home town', after many years in the avant-garde wilderness producing 'fragmented' images that 'reflected the visually splintered character of Los Angeles' street scene'. But –

> Now Gehry favors cohesion over fragmentation. As he grows older he seems to believe that the center can

hold, that the energies that glue things together may, after all, be strong enough to counter the forces of disintegration.

'After years of breaking things apart, I'm trying to put Humpty Dumpty together again', Gehry said. 'A sign of maturity?' Maybe . . .[53]

In this article, written for as many different audiences as Gehry had to address in his design, one finds the archetypal justifications necessary in a pluralist society. First references to culture, then civic space, then the power structure and its representatives, then an appeal to functionalism and populism; finally cultural integration and the simultaneous coming of age, or coming into unity, of the architect himself. Many of these points are exemplary and very much worth supporting. But the assumption of cultural unity is severely challenged by the different ways the design is perceived, the various perceptual codes, the existing pluralism.

A slew of letters to the *Los Angeles Times*, published under the heading 'Disney Hall: "Work of Art" or Wet Cardboard?', contested the judgement and metaphors of Whiteson. Several writers found the building 'ugly'; not a 'galleon in full sail' but 'deconstructionist trash', or 'cardboard boxes inhabited by the homeless'. One writer saw the joyful shapes as a 'playful child with tongue stuck out', another as 'a fortune cookie gone berserk', a third as 'a clump of trash in the gutter of Los Angeles', a fourth as 'a pile of broken crockery from an archeological dig', a fifth as 'a pile of rain-soaked cardboard dumped unceremoniously from a trash truck', a sixth, again, as an 'emptied . . . waste basket', a seventh, again, as 'a wet cardboard box', and so on. The negative metaphors took the wind out of Whiteson's billowing sails.[54] Then Gehry's supporters rallied with their counter-images and counter-attacks on the Philistines, while one self-confessed Philistine reporter took a straw-pole at his local bar and, no surprise, found that most of the tipplers hated the design. They compared it to the results of a 'tornado', a 'wax building left in the sun', or 'Downtown after The Big One'.[55]

What conclusions come from such disjunctions in taste and judgement? Obviously in a heterogeneous culture when a public building is presented as an object of cultural unity it will be immediately contested. No matter how well designed the architecture, the assertion of a unifying gesture will invite dissent, and the

*OPPOSITE: (62) Disney Hall streetside foyer breaks through the masonry, visually connecting automobile-city and high culture. Originally Gehry wanted an even more open 'living-room for the city', but various functional – and perhaps even security – considerations lessened the glazed areas. The curved French limestone, computer designed and cut to avoid waste, undulates softly like Gehry's Vitra Museum, the latest version of his new vermiform grammar. (Joshua White)*

more original the design the greater the possible disagreements, because it challenges convention and the new forms allow each different interest group to find some confirmation of its particular reading. Thus, because of the original fractured shapes, it *does* make sense to see the design as a 'wet cardboard box' and 'deconstructionist trash' if one is predisposed against the architectural avant-garde. Such readings are coherent and relate to some aspects of the form, even if they are one-sided and inadequate.

Every assertion of cultural unity is a pretext for new divisions; such is the price of a vital pluralism. But this confrontation of values, and codes of perception, is precisely the ideal of an open society. John Stuart Mill, in his classic essay *On Liberty*, 1859, put the case for the 'salutary effect' of a 'collision of opinions'.

> Not violent conflict between parts of the truth, but the quiet suppression of half of it is the formidable evil; there is always hope when people are forced to listen to both sides; it is when they attend to only one that errors harden into prejudices . . .

So the architecture of an open society must articulate opposite opinions and 'listen to both sides'; as we have seen, the principle of double-coding is essential to a dialogic which is open-ended and oriented to a future world. The Disney Hall design is both 'a galleon in full sail' *and* reminiscent of Schnabel's 'broken crockery', as well as a series of other metaphors. These lead to many new readings and push me to a prediction.

### ET UNUM ET PLURA

When the design is finally built, and used for several years, I believe its inventive forms will invite still different and deeper understandings. It is impossible to say exactly what these might be, but some of their overtones may be divined. The gently rising white forms of the outside, like the up-curves of a Chinese roof, are bound to be read as anthropomorphic gestures – perhaps not exactly 'smiles' as the Chinese convention has it – but something as generally cheerful and uplifting as going to a musical performance is supposed to be (63). The festive occasion of a night out is captured here and Gehry has quite consciously conceived his white limestone curves and counter-curves in the way they will be perceived at night. Light will break

*OPPOSITE (63) Disney Hall, a festive counterpoint of mostly up-turned forms, which lean outwards. The glazed protrusions set up a secondary theme and at night, during most concerts, will bounce shafts of light across the limestone surface. (Joshua White)*

through the voids, inviting concert-goers to explore all parts of the site, pulling them into the garden terraces and around the sides of the building. Since nothing is quite predictable, the sense of mystery and discovery is heightened. Nooks and crannies will provoke constant surprise. Contrast this with the adjacent, sub-classical Music Center, and the virtue of this open-architecture is clear. The former coherently suggests many divergent metaphors of music, play and growth, while the latter reductively fixates on a sombre experience of culture, the rectitude of going to church, the discipline of the temple.

If the outside can be a 'white rose', a 'galleon', a 'crushed box' and 'broken crockery' all at once, the inside continues to develop the nautical imagery. Hans Scharoun's Berlin Philharmonic Hall, the expressionist concert hall of the 1960s, was one prototype Gehry looked at which also uses ship imagery, and 'vineyards of people', to distribute the audience. But Gehry's internal 'Noah's Ark' is much tighter and tauter than Scharoun's; its white acoustic sails push down deeper into the central space, giving it a real focus and drama (63, 64). The space billows out at the four corners which are also back lit and this, combined with the outward tilt of the walls, invites one to explore the back and the ceiling of the hall. It is this suggestion to go beyond what one can see that is so crucial to the design as a whole. By cutting volumes up, layering and back-lighting them, Gehry creates a strong sense of anticipation and surprise at every point. Yet the scheme is never entirely chaotic, nor are the entrance and exits a mystery, as they often are in expressionist cultural centres (the Hayward Gallery and Queen Elizabeth Hall in London are typical rabbit-warrens). One can immediately sense the overall order of the lower foyer and the four-square concert hall. As with other Gehry designs, there is a very simple and sensible solution underlying a seemingly complex, fragmented geometry.

It may be too soon to say, as Whiteson does, that the building is a masterpiece, but I do think it bears comparison with other multivalent buildings such as Le Corbusier's Ronchamp and Jorn Utzon's Sydney Opera House. Like them it suggests without naming, and offers a coherent and internally resolved set of new forms, which provoke imaginative readings. This sets the mind off on a game of 'hunt the symbol', where it always comes up with several different solutions, all of them correct. If Ronchamp was the opening bar of post-modern jive in 1955, then Disney Hall will be one of its primary recapitulations in 1995. It is an equally well-crafted counterpoint of enigmatic forms. Such precise resolutions took Gehry more than thirty models.

Obviously a single public building cannot bring a heterogeneous culture together any more than it can heal the wounds of the riot. It is vain to ask art or architecture to make up for political, economic or social inadequacy. Yet it still makes sense to ask a public building to symbolize a credible public realm, to set a relevant direction and act as if its meaning could be universalized for society at this time and place. For Los Angleles and for the rest of America this means a particularly heterogeneous, minoritized culture where no one architectural language – traditional, classical, Anglo-Saxon or Hispanic – is dominant and uncontested. By the year 2050 demographers predict the county will be more than fifty per cent non-white – as it was for the first fifteen thousand years of its occupation by *homo sapiens*. It is probably the case, because of political turmoil and mass migrations, that most world cities will have many of the ethnic problems, and advantages, that Los Angeles enjoys today. So in an important sense it is the archetypal global city of the future.

Given the increasing pluralism, Gehry's Disney Hall, and hetero-architecture in general, are intelligent responses for an open situation. They are sufficiently abstract not to legitimize *any* subculture: Anglo, colonial or whatever remains the dominant visual language of America, except of course modernism, which promotes abstraction as an official style. The group of modernists still remain something of a leading professional tribe within the AIA.

But hetero-architecture is also representational and metaphorical in all sorts of ways that make contact with the public at large, and in this sense they challenge the modernist dominance as well. Truly post-modern, their doubly-coded discourse inscribes *and* subverts social meaning at the same time – the definition of a 'poetics of post-modernism', as Linda Hutcheon (and I) have been pointing out for some time.[56] Its agenda is to transcend or contest divisions in taste, to overcome institutional and linguistic barriers that fracture contemporary culture. The poetics of post-modernism are radically eclectic, inclusive of any discourse that is locally relevant and of modernism itself.

But this approach is also particularly relevant to heterogeneous America as a whole, as it tries to reinvent a new public self-image. *E pluribus unum*, 'out of many, one', is no longer quite adequate, since this unity has all-too-often meant the values and tastes of the dominant culture, or, even worse, a faceless corporatism. The 'melting pot' as a metaphor is no longer accepted. The 'boiling pot', its antithesis, also misses what immigrants and their host country want: neither the bland homogeneity of Middle America, nor the fractious disjunctions of separate ethnic ghettoes. Other images and models, such as a 'mosaic or kaleidoscope of subcultures', comes closer to what is desired by both sides. This is a situation where immigrants assimilate in some ways – economically, legally, technically – and still remain culturally distinct. Culture is, in the end, what makes life worth living – the peculiar values, customs, ideas and religious practices which are always historical. In this sense all those who have something to contribute are already what the Korean said he would always be: a 'hyphenated-American', a hybrid of the local and universal, the past and present.

If this is true – and I realize some people will prefer to call themselves 'American-Americans' – then it would entail a sensitivity to difference *at the same time* as social unity is proposed: a representation of unity *and* dissent, *et unum et plura*, the one *and* the many. The debate on multiculturalism has foundered because one side of this dialogue is always promoted at the expense of the other: classical Western civilization versus ethnic culture, assimilation versus difference. The antinomies are too well known to need rehashing. We understand the arguments and are tired of the caricatures such as 'political correctness'.

Immigrants keep coming to America. Its culture is vital, not only because of this long-standing argument but also because it can be transcended as the battle between the one and the many, the *unum* and *plura*, and displaced to a third category: invention. The interesting fact of creativity, as the Disney Hall and so many other inventive, heterogeneous artifacts show, is to make conflict lead not to destruction, but an entirely 'other' situation that none of the contestants had imagined. Poised between fracture and a new culture, Los Angeles seems like the rest of America writ small: on the verge of either splitting up or of making something strange and exciting that no one has seen before.

*OPPOSITE: (64) Disney Hall interior. Two thousand three hundred and fifty concert-goers are suspended around a central orchestra, over which hangs a cascade of descending acoustic sails. Mr Nagata, a Japanese acoustician, worked with Gehry on sixty different solutions, and together they finally came up with the downwardly curving ceiling, outwardly leaning walls, and indirect light at four corners drawing the eye upwards and outwards. (Brian S Yoo)*

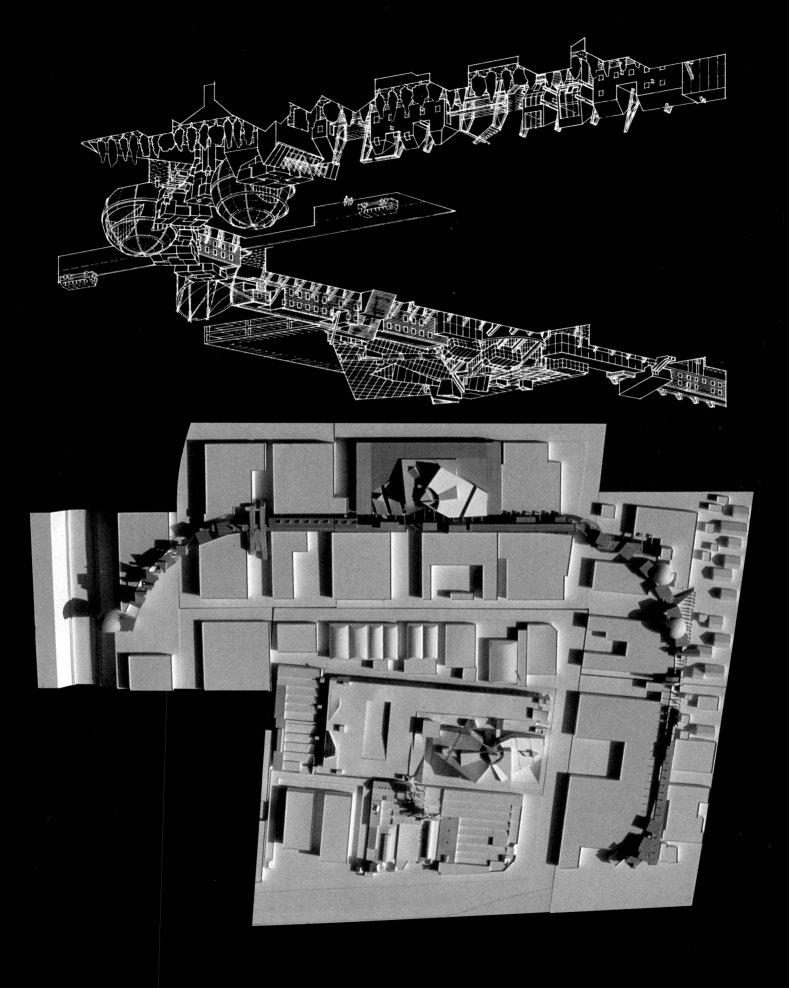

# CHAPTER SIX

# TOWARDS A POST-MODERN LIBERALISM

Los Angeles has grown like Topsy into *the* multicultural city with more variety of flora, fauna, lifestyles, ethnic groups and individuals doing their own thing – with more sheer difference – than any other city I know. Yet all global cities are going in the same direction, the result of mass migration, increasing trade and expanding communication. Often a culture creates itself, like an individual, without being fully in control of its own growth and direction. Sudden events, switches in direction, as well as processes working below consciousness, lead to a structure which no one intends.

However, to some degree the United States has shaped its growth since the Enlightenment, establishing a set of rules and customs which has nurtured a heterogeneous society. The Constitution and the Bill of Rights guarantee certain fundamental rights that encourage diversity: free speech, assembly, due process, free practice of religion, equality before the law and so on. These canons and regulations constituted Modern Liberalism and were significant particularly because they were abstract. To be considered fair, they had to be 'universal' and blind to color, creed, class, gender, age – indeed to all the differences which divide people. Supposedly they lead to a justice which is 'blind', to the separation of church and state and, in the U.S., to the careful avoidance of state support for the good life as seen by one ethnic group rather than another.

But such abstract 'right' and the proposition that 'all men are created equal', it turns out, are not, as the framers of the Constitution claimed, 'natural'. After all, everything in nature is created unequal except such things as electrons which are, indeed, absolutely identical. Even these entities differ radically the minute they become part of a particular, historical atom in a certain molecule, so the notion of equality as identity is an abstraction even in physics.

Nonetheless the United States, and many liberal democracies following it, have assumed natural justice as both an underlying process and normative goal, and thereby furthered a very real liberating history. The notion of fundamental rights is now accepted

*OPPOSITE: (65) Eric Owen Moss, S.P.A.R.C.I.T.Y. project for Culver City, Los Angeles, 1992-. The architectural equivalent of Post-Modern Liberalism sets up a dialogue between the universal and local, in this case the pre-existing city fabric (mostly abandoned warehouses) different zones (industrial, commercial, residential, civic) and the new linear attachments (add-ons, refurbishments, piggy-back buildings of different use). The goal of post-modern urbanism is to regenerate a declining city with functions that hybridize the usually separate zones. The city is now studying the project's feasibility. (T. Conversano)*

by much of the world and in 1982 was extended by the United Nations to the biosphere and all life forms: 'every form of life is unique, warranting respect regardless of its worth to man.'[57] The liberal-ecological injunction could not be more clear: treat every living thing as an end in itself, not just as an instrument of human value. This 'politics of universalism', as Charles Taylor so aptly elucidates it, is now being challenged by a 'politics of difference.'[58] The reasons are well known but nevertheless worth summarizing.

It has now become apparent, through psychological and cultural studies, that personal identity is largely constructed in dialogue with others. I have already mentioned Mikhail Bakhtin's important theories of dialogic, an idea which is also central to Charles Taylor's argument for a new politics of recognition. The formative nature of dialogue has also been emphasized by such post-modern writers as the theologian Martin Buber and the physicist David Bohm. Some unexpected truths flow from these theories. Since the Enlightenment, since Rousseau and the Romantics, a paramount value has been placed on individual self-development and individual morality. 'Listen to your own inner voice' is one typical injunction or, as Polonius advised Laertes: 'To thine own self be true, And it must follow, as the night the day, Thou cans't not then be false to any man'. The idea is now accepted by almost everyone. Moral and aesthetic judgement must come from within, not just from external guidelines such as the Ten Commandments or a code of behavior.

The same standards of creativity and self-reflection apply in the aesthetic world: a new work of art or architecture must be appropriate in some way which entails reflection, otherwise it will not be accepted as valuable and significant. Hence an axiology of inwardness and sensitivity to subjective feelings has grown over the last three centuries, resulting in quite opposite events: a plethora of modern art movements and a subculture of 'do your own thing'; existentialist individualism and the 'me generation'; L.A. ersatz and creative difference. The discourses of individualism have created ambivalent results and a balance sheet equally weighted between creativity and inanity.

The surprising contribution of dialogic (and some other social sciences) to the debate on individualism is to show how much of the self is constructed socially: in dialogue with others. Contrary to the Romantic notion that the subject must generate itself just from within, it now appears that the individual creates an inner voice through different dialogues with a series of what George Herbert Mead calls 'significant others'.[59] The greater the number of dialogues, the more frames of reference from which to savor and judge reality. No language, according to this theory, means no self, no inner voices contending, debating and celebrating. Perhaps most surprisingly this dialogue can occur with non-material entities: a possible future audience for Vincent van Gogh, an ideal Russia for Aleksander Solzhenitsyn, western literature conceived as a whole for T.S. Eliot, and God for a hermit. Social construction of the self can, paradoxically, exist without a functioning society.

But in most cases, and for most of one's life, positive identity is shaped through dialogue in which others recognize one's distinctive voice and vice versa. Because of this, the 'politics of recognition', as Taylor calls it, is not a piety, but a *necessity* for human development. According to this theory, the greatest damage one can do to an individual, and group, is to suppress a language, or even be insensitive to its particular virtues. Benign neglect, according to this orientation, is in fact malign neglect. The strong point of the multiculturalist argument is that when dialogue is withheld, or when a group's identity is treated contemptuously, those who are marginalized internalize a diminished view of themselves. The worst oppression, according to this view, is self-oppression, the feelings of inadequacy built into the reigning discourses and absorbed, without anyone intending it, by the minorities. Since any culture, even the supposedly universal liberal democracies, must favor a set of languages, customs, and assumptions, they inevitably suppress other values. While the U.S. Constitution claims to uphold a justice which is blind to color and ethnicity, it implicitly supports the Anglo-Saxon Protestantism and language from which it is derived. These truths become apparent on State occasions such as the inauguration of a President or the burial of a statesman. Regardless of the theory, in fact the playing field is never flat. The dominant culture always skews the 'universals' towards its own self-interest and identity.

It is this deep truth – a consequence of the dialogical nature of identity – which can lead to an unconscious hypocrisy, galling to the rest of the world when the United States claims to act on behalf of abstract rights, which, so clearly to others, are tacit Anglo values. The disagreements are made yet more convoluted by the fact that the U.S. is a 'nation-state of many nations' and because this active pluralism is an implicit rebuke to so many countries trying to become more democratic. Others love to hate it: on one hand, it is not impartial enough and always puts its self-interest first; on the other hand, it is still considerably more tolerant of difference than most countries.

Such contradictions and complexities raise an intractable problem. As Charles Taylor argues, it is based on two different versions of liberalism: the politics of universalism (what I have called Modern Liberalism) out of which has grown the politics of difference. Modernists, with their institutionalization of abstract rights, developed the first, and it is now a question of whether post-modernists can combine it with the second in a new 'politics of recognition'. Certainly after two hundred years of building a legal and state system on fundamental rights, it is possible to add to them some cultural rights of recognition. The time for this interweaving may be ripe; the debate on multiculturalism presupposes that it is.

The solution that Taylor and his supporters have come to is an interesting blend of the two liberalisms which is situation-dependent. They argue that a nation-state like Norway, Holland or France, or a nation within a nation-state like Quebec, can adopt policies that discriminate in favor of one culture as long as they do not infringe fundamental rights, particularly those of minorities. Such positive discrimination will only exist *sometimes*, in certain defined areas, such as favoring the French language in *some* Quebec schools where there are a preponderance of French speakers, and this discrimination has to be made on a case by case basis. In other words the policy of cultural recognition will be situational and assumed to operate with a different logic than abstract rights.

A significant point is that the conflict between the two liberalisms is presumed to be basic, like the long-standing frictions between liberty and equality, prosperity and justice, private property and the biosphere. It would be a better-designed universe if these different positive values were not in opposition. They do tend to conflict, however, and a gain in one is usually offset by a loss in the other. Recognizing such contradictions, and the compromises which stem from them, requires a certain kind of sensibility and maturity, which post-modernists believe should characterize our time. For instance, to return to architecture, Robert Venturi proffers a 'complexity and contradiction' which owes an 'obligation towards the difficult whole', a whole which includes conflicting parts.

How very real and necessary this sensibility is can be seen in the multicultural school system of Los Angeles, where thousands of new immigrants are absorbed every year and many languages are spoken. As the intake of different ethnic groups goes up, the normal educational standards may go down, especially if, as during the Reagan years, the schools are starved of funds. For instance, Fairfax High School dropped from the top twenty-five per cent of the schools statewide to the bottom quarter as its ethnic diversity rose during the period 1980-1990. This does not prove that cultural pluralism and good exam results are incompatible, but there is enough corroborative evidence to suggest that, in a declining economic situation, the two values may necessitate a trade-off. Presently nearly forty per cent of the students are Latino, twenty-nine per cent white (including a substantial number of Armenian and Russian immigrants) fifteen per cent are black, twelve per cent Asian, 3.4 per cent Filipino, and less than one per cent Pacific Islander and Native American. The numbers of whites and blacks have declined substantially in the past twenty years as the Latinos and Asians have risen.

In January 1993 an accidental fatal shooting of a student brought this multicultural and educational issue to the fore. Interestingly the principal of the school, the teachers and the students all came to the defense of pluralism. Even after the shooting they acknowledged the virtues of learning from diversity. One student said, 'there are good things and bad things at every school, but I wouldn't trade my school for anything'. Another was more explicit on the point: 'I go to a school where I get to know people from all over the world. I would rather come here than a place where I didn't meet other types of people'.[60] In other words, students particularly appreciate the point of the trade-off: a decline in test-scores is partly compensated for by a gain in cultural variety and differing viewpoints. One also learns from the latter. The dominant notion of a normal education is challenged by these opinions. Conservatives, who usually deplore the lowering of standards, nevertheless have to admit that the schools are a main place where immigrants learn English and assimilate Anglo culture. If we are going to recognize them as a major site where the problems of multiculturalism are played out, it follows that school funding should be increased rather than be cut.

Acknowledging rather than denying such conflicts between two different goals – conventional education geared to exam results and education through differenĉe – is a precondition for avoiding the sacrifice of one to the other in the usual politics of polarization. It requires more tension than the models of cultural integration provide, whether traditional or modern, because it calls for the ability to hold contradictory moralities in suspension. That a high school student understands this immediately shows how deeply valued multiculturalism has become today. More than is commonly acknowledged, we are all natural pluralists with an inherent attraction to variety. We already know what post-modern theories are trying to establish: that we learn through understanding both similarity and difference and the dialogue between them.

### HETEROPOLIS NOT COSMOPOLIS

Underlying the modern/post-modern debate are various assumptions which suggest it cannot be resolved. Foremost among them is a binary logic which requires that if one is right the other is wrong. Often the debate is framed as an opposition between Western culture and immigrant cultures: in education, a core curriculum of Plato, Shakespeare, Darwin and the one hundred great books set against works by authors who are non-white, non-male and non-Western. According to the logic of limited time and money, if one side of this binary pair is cultivated the other is curtailed. According to dialogic, if minority culture is not taught and respected, minorities in the West will inevitably continue to have a diminished self-image.

Arguments on both sides clearly make sense and lead to contradictory conclusions: one cannot cut the teaching of Western culture without lowering standards but at the same time one must augment the teaching of non-Western culture to give minorities recognition essential to their identity. Put in this way, the contradiction results in a zero-sum game and eternal conflict: victories for one side will always be losses for the other.

With this vicious choice we best revert to the rabbi's proverbial advice to his son: 'Whenever faced with two extremes, always pick a third'. In this case the other position, outside the either/or debate, assumes that identity is always already eclectic. If children are naturally pluralists and find a spontaneous pleasure in experiencing difference, then so too are those brought up in multicultural societies when they have not learned prejudice, or when they have not been suppressed. Ethnic hatred has to be nurtured, as it is in Belfast, Jerusalem and other notable cities of perennial battle. But in many heteropolitan cities where variety is accepted until there is an imposed ethnic strife – the previously multi-ethnic Sarajevo is typical – pluralism is experienced as a gain for all sides.

The United States, founded in part on the idea that difference can be a positive sum game, has inevitably created a citizenry that takes pleasure in broadening its experience to include alien tastes within its identity. That is to say it has created compound identities whose very being consists in reaching across ethnic divides. This may extend from minor pleasures – consuming different cuisines and playing a variety of national sports – to reading various literatures, to a taste for hearing opposite opinions and enjoying sudden juxtapositions in mood and thought. In other words, the argument for multicultural identity cuts two different ways. It can support an ethnic reductivism, where a minority culture is sympathetically nurtured and, at the same time, give aid to a nation of heteropolitan citizens who nonetheless carry their old-world culture on their backs.

Such underlying hybridization leads to a third position outside the polarizations of the conservatives versus the multiculturalists, the essentialists versus the deconstructivists and – combined with the lessons of hetero-architecture – it leads to some unexpected conclusions. Ethnicity, like a restricted language such as mathematics, is an interesting double-bind: it both liberates and ensnares individuals, ties them to a community and allows them to create an identity. As Anglo-Saxon ethnicity has become more diffuse in the United States over three hundred years, as it has become generalized by Middle America and commercialized by such corporate industries as Ralph Lauren Inc, it has positively opened up the culture to other influences, but negatively has left a void which many North Americans fill with all sorts of partial practices: spiritualism, a search for 'roots', self-improvement regimes and a thousand individualizing and grounding pursuits.

To a degree the same process is underway in all First World cultures that are subject to a global commercialism often perceived as 'Americanization'. One can foresee this global, corporate culture becoming a dominant in the EC, Japan, South East Asia and perhaps the former communist world. Many would claim there is already a world-wide Western meta-culture, of a very approximate kind. They point to such events as the 1989 uprising in Tiananmen Square, Peking. During months of demonstrating the students mixed quotes from Mao with phrases from the French and American Revolutions, they sang Chinese songs and Beethoven's 'Ode to Joy'; they borrowed ideas from Confucius and the Bill of Rights; and their symbolic rallying point was a sculpture which mixed the American

Statue of Liberty with the French Liberté called 'The Goddess of Democracy'. All this hybridization was amplified by CNN, fax machines and other communicational aids, and was produced for the global media to rebroadcast. A world-wide electronic culture, as it could be called, is likely to become much more pervasive with creative and authentic, if tragic, examples such as Tiananmen Square. By contrast, a large amount of media-events will be tribal celebrations such as Royal Weddings (and divorces). Will such commercialization make ethnicity an embarrassment?

This may lead, as it has in the U.S., to a further diffusion and slackening of traditional symbols and values – to the point where either they have no power or they become more disguised. To a degree Middle America has substituted lifestyles for ethnicity, a process which the maps (pages 26-31) bring out: consumption patterns have overlaid inherited customs, chosen tastes have subsumed traditional values. This melange has become the reigning background culture. There is probably no global solution to this general slackening, and all attempts to direct culture as a whole have, in this century, usually destroyed it. But piecemeal programs such as support for local cultures, and particular measures, such as support for the French language in parts of Quebec, are obviously desirable. In addition, some modest lessons from the hetero-architecture of Los Angeles bear on the general issue. I will summarize them starting from the least contentious.

First, and most obvious, is the notion of contextualism as seen in the work of Charles Moore and Robert Venturi. These two post-modernists confront the history of a place and the tastes of a subculture directly. For them the context of architecture includes the surrounding environment and the particular symbols of a real community, and they do not shy away from representing these 'embarrassing' signs whether they happen to be a UCLA bear outside the Medical Research Laboratories (35, 36), or the local brick and stone grammar or the aedicules of a Protestant church (22). Conventional signs are renewed through transformation into a new contextual grammar, but they are still recognizable. In a sense this accessibility is the key for what Charles Taylor calls the politics of recognition, for if a culture or ethnic group cannot appreciate its symbols directly then it will imagine them to be private, not worthy of public expression. The problem with explicit symbolism is that it often becomes a sign that is easily exploited commercially. The represen-

*(66) Barton Myers, Center for the Performing Arts, Cerritos, Los Angeles, 1989-93. Different materials and shapes articulate the various functions and regional codes in a manner which stresses difference. The communal meeting hall can be seen to the right, the entrance lobby surmounted by 'Cerritos blue' tile is in the center and the main auditorium is to the left. Great variety of material and form dramatizes an inclusive aesthetic. The interior auditorium – which can be easily altered into five different configurations – accommodates opposite kinds of performance and thus provides a space and amenity for the different ethnic groups and taste-cultures. Film, dance, large-scale dramas, musicals, political rallies, conferences, concerts and virtually any small-scale public function can occur here. Radical eclecticism mirrors the radical inclusiveness. (Tim Street Porter, photograph courtesy of the architect)*

tational hetero-architecture of theme parks and L.A. ersatz has so dismayed some local architects that they would go to any lengths of incomprehensibility to avoid the possible taint of 'kitsch'.

A way of surmounting this problem is by combining signs and symbols so they compete with each other and avoid the endorsement of a single world-view. Weak eclecticism is the trusted method of Disneyland, but a more radical variety – practiced by Moore, Venturi and lately by Barton Myers – looks for justification of literal symbols in local materials, local climate and particular functions. In this sense it is a direct outgrowth of the regional Modernism proffered by Frank Lloyd Wright, Bay Area designers and even, in his East Coast work, the ultra-internationalist Walter Gropius. Vernacular usage or what Charles Moore calls 'readily available materials' – that is industrial vernacular – is the ubiquitous rationale. From Schindler's wood frame and stucco to Gehry's 'cheapskate aesthetic' of chain-link, every California architect has probably justified a choice of form-language this way. Again there are dangers as well as problems of banality: what material and structural system cannot today be purchased locally? However, eclecticism can be deepened, as Moore's St Matthews' Parish Church shows, when there is a real interaction between architect and users, when they challenge each other with their own desires and expertise. Participatory design has been a piety of the profession since the 1960s and it can lead to cost-overruns and design by committee; but it is a *sine qua non* which guarantees nothing. Without it the result is 'architect's architecture', with it there is the possibility of greater resonance and creativity but no guarantee of authentic architecture.

The idea that some process, or set of guidelines such as those proposed here, will naturally result in beneficent design is one of the pipe dreams fostered by the modernist commitment to 'right method'. But if there is one thing apparent in these post-modern times it is that architecture is not just a skill, like swimming, that can be learned once and for all. Rather, as John Turner has phrased it, architecture is a verb, indeed an existentially demanding verb that asks for risk and commitment by the architect and community. Society has institution-alized the hope that we can sub-contract existential commitment and have a genius, or star architect, do the creativity and heart-work for us. Yet if architecture is a transitive verb, like politics and religion, it makes no more sense to suppose a professional can do it alone than it does to believe politicians will go in certain directions without constant public pressure, or that religious leaders can spiritually heal society or create mystical experiences for others. As Matthew Fox says, in another context, 'you can't rent a mystic, not even in California'. Architecture, at least great architecture, also demands personal and collective engagement. It cannot be bought off the shelf or produced by a machine, however thoughtfully programed.

'The architecture of good intentions', as Colin Rowe called modernist utopias, paved over enough roads to that well known place. Hence the prescriptions offered here are given with some caveats and irony. Whatever method, or style, or set of values is adopted in a global culture, it tends to become a caricature of its inspiration and a new part of the problem. In spite of this it is still important to propose general principles that face up to the multicultural and ecological realities, although with a hindsight focused on modernist failures regarding the inadequacy of good intentions and right methods (principles which served an ideological function to expand the architectural profession), it becomes ambiguous to do so. As Umberto Eco puts it, post-modernists live in an 'age of lost inno cence' where they know that positive prescriptions may well turn into clichés, so that they cannot be offered with anything less than a warning and irony.

This brings us to a more contentious aspect of hetero-architecture, the question of double-coding. If there are two distinct and contradictory moralities underlying the debate – the politics of universalism and the politics of difference – then the architect as much as the politician must weave them together and, at times, confront both. The conflict cannot be dissolved by any Rousseauian 'general will', or 'good of the whole', or, as it usually appears in architecture, 'organicism'. The desire for an organic society and organic architecture goes back to Aristotle and forward to Alberti, Frank Lloyd Wright, Walter Gropius and the present-day ecologists, all of whom have explicitly asked for various types of holistic building and cultural integration. Indeed the aesthetic and juridical drive towards unity has been a constant of Western culture since Plato, and it makes a certain sense in a small, isolated community which has been culturally unified for generations. However, in large pluralistic cities the attempt to impose, or promote, such integration will always be perceived by the minorities as a form of implicit domination. Hence the constant post-modern injunction, as Jean-François Lyotard put it, of 'a war on totality' – or, as I prefer it, the necessity for double-coding.

In designing for a community one must assume the conflict of at least two major languages: the local and universal, the particular and technological, the historical and modern. There are many more discourses than these but they tend to cluster into binary pairs. Frank Gehry's Chiat/Day/Mojo office plays the Venice beach signs – boat, trees and fish – against the technological and practical – the architecture of industrial fixtures and sheet metal. Eric Owen Moss and Frank Israel, in their warehouse conversions, contrast the village with the high-tech contraption, as well as the previous building with a new insertion. There is nothing peaceful or holistic in these contrasts. On the contrary, non-integration is dramatized, which leads to the question: what is the 'obligation to the difficult whole'? If two different codes are always represented, and the grand contradiction between the universal and ethnic is reified, then are the cultural divisions not being exacerbated? This seems to me an open question. Double-coding acknowledges the major fracture of our time and represents it back to society, saying in effect: 'Your values and tastes are opposed to each other but equally worthy of presentation. What happens next is important – whether some form of fusion takes place or not – that the dialogue is recognized and engaged.'

There is a parallel in the debate on multiculturalism. One must approach non-Western cultures, Charles Taylor argues, with the presumption of equal worth, but not with one's mind made up that they are the same, or of equal value, in all respects. To avoid falling into a form of inverted cultural condescension, as bad as the old, one has to be prepared for judgements of inequality, the constant give and take of dialogue which presumes a generalized respect but also an indeterminate outcome. In a respectful meeting of unequals both sides will gain and lose and be changed. If they go on communicating then perhaps, in the best cases, a 'fusion of horizons' will prevail, an unforced synthesis. The architect's obligation is to set the precondition for this synthesis, not assume it has occurred, and this means honoring and representing the two discourses on their own terms.

The most contentious implication of hetero-architecture, or at least the best of it, is that there are 'universal', transcendent and cosmic qualities which can be represented. In the introduction I alluded to the spiritual dimension of a living language of architecture. This is something that cannot be directly represented, only presented. Talk about spiritual values notoriously betray them because they are often best conveyed by activity and, like sexual attraction and artistic grace, they are operative or not; analyzing their virtues may well drive them out. In spite of this tendency a few things can be said.

The Los Angeles School of architects, particularly Frank Gehry, has demonstrated an old truth of architecture, that it often pays to stick close to the informal, the banal and the everyday – if these conditions can be made to release their unsuspected potential. There is usually a strange beauty to be discovered in the necessary and the given, but it will not reveal itself unless provoked. Everyone hates chain-link fence, but as Gehry noticed, it tends to grow like an unwanted fungus around Los Angeles buildings because it is cheap and socially necessary. His insight occurred when designing a second story porch for his three-year-old son to play outside under, without falling to the ground. A simple chain-link surround would be a cage, but a series of flying webs of steel might create a new aesthetic of changing *moire* patterns and a quite 'other' situation. Why name this new space, if it has no pre-existence? But 'cage' it is not. Chain-link is treated as scrim, as a gauze of shimmering steel squares which, when overlapping with each other, create new unexpected rhythms and chaotic zones. The order out of chaos emerges quite naturally, unasked for, if one simply doubles or triples the disagreeable material. Banal in its original state, it becomes extraordinary when re-used this way. All of the L.A. School have discovered such minor but significant new usages in modest materials and unpromising situations, an approach I have called 'en-formality' to underline its unlikely combination of informality and oddness. It is now a self-conscious style, as ubiquitous in Los Angeles as the palm tree. The work illustrated, insofar as it creatively extends an informal language of architecture, presents a spirituality in action.

There is another transcendent aspect to this architecture which deserves comment. If the appreciation of difference and otherness is quite spontaneous, like curiosity, and just as deeply rooted in the psyche as the desire to identify with an ethnic group or tribe, then it can develop paradoxically into its own form of identity. People who are confident about their background, and not particularly threatened by another group's powers, can actually take delight in their differences, in seeing the world through other mentalities, in experiencing other sets of customs and classifications of things. This taste for otherness may even extend to preferring different opinions to one's own – which are, after all, slightly boring because one knows

*(67 & 68) Frank Gehry, Edgemar Farms Conversion, Santa Monica, 1987-9. Chain Link transformed, softened, exploited for its* moire *patterns, its emergent order and chaos.*

them. The Marquis de Sade said nothing is so enjoyable as a shock to the nervous system, a truth well known to children. Travel, mountain climbing and reading novels all testify to this natural drive.

A few cities in the past, such as Alexandria, or today Rome and London, have based their economies and everyday life on nurturing a culture of heterogeneity. They have welcomed, or tolerated, foreign tribes within their poleis, sometimes as equal trading partners, sometimes as exploited 'guest workers', sometimes as long-term residents or short-term tourists. Whatever the motives, the notion of the cosmopolis has been accepted as one desirable model of the world city since the time of the Romans, and today it is the possible essential definition of New York, San Francisco, Berlin, Frankfurt, Hong Kong, Tokyo, Amsterdam, Paris and perhaps forty other leading centers of the global economy.

While desirable in many respects, there are at least two fundamental problems to this type of city. As attacks on cosmopolitanism suggest, it can lead to various forms of economic exploitation. Individuals and groups, multinationals and 'global tribes', as they are known, can feed off the host economy , export their profits, and give back nothing to the locale. Secondly, and related to this exploitation, is the question of rootlessness. The pluralist philosopher Isaiah Berlin, in an interview on the rise of contemporary nationalism, put the case succinctly:

> My hero Herder said: 'cosmopolitans are empty people, they are loyal to nothing, they have no ideas' – Yes, I am against cosmopolitanism. Internationalism is an admirable idea, but for that you need nations, between whom there are alliances, combinations, agreements and peace treaties – that, yes. But cosmopolitanism is the deprivation of human beings, of their [legitimate] wishing to belong, and that would impoverish them.[61]

A cosmopolite, by definition at home in all parts of the world, free from local attachments and prejudices, is also by definition bereft of commitments to a particular ecology and way of life.

This ambivalence makes the concept of the heteropolis more acceptable than the cosmopolis. The enjoyment of difference and variety in a city makes it necessary that one respects and furthers the 'otherness' one finds, gives something back to the pre-existing heterogeneity. The long-term goal of the heteropolis, its defining goal, is not only to sustain itself as a viable economic and ecological entity, but to further a slow, peaceful interweaving of world-views. Such intermixtures can only take place when there is a true dialogue between cultures: neither coercion nor domination of one by another, but a sustained relationship of talking and listening, sometimes painful, sometimes enjoyable.

Unless one emphasizes the pleasure and creativity basic to the hybrid culture, the whole project of a heteropolis, and a city like Los Angeles, becomes insupportably heavy, just another set of moral and economic problems to be solved – or run away from. The pleasures of a heteropolis are reward enough for facing the difficulties. The hetero-architecture of Los Angeles reminds us of a truth that has been obscured by all the ethnic strife which dominates the news today, that difference can be transformed from a pretext for conflict into an opportunity for pleasurable creativity – the invention of something beautiful or striking not known before. And that transformation is supremely sensible, sensuous and enjoyable.

The fact that ethnic identity and the self-determination of communities are fundamental issues of our time hardly needs stating. From Bosnia to Somalia, from Ireland to Moldavia, from Tibet to South Africa to Iraq to Sri Lanka, the same desire for a new politics of recognition overwhelms the previous enforced peace. The end of the Cold War has allowed long-suppressed wishes to come to the fore and, given the highly mobile and communicating world, no set of superpowers will be able to contain them. Today there are some forty-eight interethnic disputes in a total of one hundred and eighty nation-states: roughly a quarter of the world is simmering, asking for new types of self-determination.[62] These are a kind of conflict which no major philosopher of the last one hundred years predicted, and they seem beyond the control of any nation, system of government or supra-national institution. Not only is Marxism unable to explain this shift in motivating forces, but so too are other ideologies such as liberal capitalism. Nationalism, ethnicism, tribalism – as well as other 'isms' in search of a politics of recognition – defy the old categories of explanation, just as they bring an era of global stability to an end. At the same time, within previous national boundaries, millions of people are on the move, fleeing persecution or seeking better jobs. In the last ten years in Western Europe, the number of immigrants seeking asylum has risen tenfold, from an annual figure of sixty thousand to seven hundred thousand in 1992.[63] Most of these are former Yugoslavs, Romanians, Turks and Sri Lankans. The numbers are likely to swell as ethnic strife spreads in the former Soviet Union.

In ten years, the entire country of Germany, like the City of Los Angeles, has received more than a million 'temporary' residents, with the population of foreigners in cities such as Berlin rising to fifteen per cent. In 1991 it was estimated that ten million legal and illegal new immigrants were attracted to a few large cities in Europe, such as London, Paris, Rome and Berlin, causing a backlash against asylum-seekers and a widespread political movement towards another 'Fortress Europe', one where ethnic purity will reinforce a possible economic fortress.[64] But this policy of the slammed door may already be too late: by early 1993 Germany had 5.2 million foreigners, France 3.6, Britain 1.8, and Switzerland 1.1 (or 16.3 per cent of its population).[65] At least in the major cities of Europe there has been a pluralization that would be extremely difficult to reverse short of adopting Fascist methods. With the populations flowing freely within EC borders, this diversity can only increase. Which way these cities go, and the direction for other growing, sprawling conurbations, has been constrained in the past by economic and political limits; today, for the first time, it is also perceived to be constrained by multicultural factors. There will obviously be many outcomes for the world city, from Beirut to San Francisco, from total breakdown to fruitful coexistence, from the cosmopolis to the heteropolis. Every large city will have some degree of choice about where it fits within this wide spectrum, but to make it an intelligent one will require an understanding of the new possibilities.

### DEEPENING THE VALUES

The pressures on the heteropolis, and Los Angeles in particular, are pushing it towards a crisis point and choice. Let me put it most starkly: unless the dominant culture acknowledges the way it suppresses different, marginal groups and, at the same time, unless these groups and the dominant culture acknowledge the way they have together suppressed the bioregions, there will not be much of a future worth worrying about. The problems of a diversifying society and environmental destruction are positively correlated. In other words, in order to survive, the heteropolis will have to comprehend more fully the two conflicting modes of justice – the politics of universalism and of difference – and to engage their values more deeply in a new set of relationships. Emergent aspects of Post-Modern Liberalism suggest what some of these relationships might be.

As the hetero-architecture of Los Angeles shows, there is a great virtue, and pleasure, to be had in mixing categories, transgressing boundaries, inverting custom and adopting the marginal usage. This approach reveals more than a desire to shock, or a taste for the *outré* in general, it is an intelligent strategy of creative hybridization, a policy of radical inclusiveness that overcomes the prevalent tendency to see things in either/or terms. Binary logic has, for too long, ruled the modern world.

According to this oppositional logic the establishment creates its anti-establishment in a two-term dialectic of winners and losers: those opposite pairs who simultaneously define each other's place in a system – and space in the city – as 'in' or 'out', dominant or subordinate, powerful or impotent. Thus the relational self-definition of white versus black, 'ethnic' versus WASP, rich versus poor, gay versus heterosexual, male versus female, skilled versus unskilled, intelligent versus uneducated, traditional versus modern. These typical oppositions are the very stuff of multicultural politics. Added to such primary pairs are a series of further oppositions which everyone experiences sometime in their life: old versus young, employed versus unemployed, body-oriented versus intellectual, emotional versus rational, religious versus agnostic, technological versus ecological, sick versus healthy. Has anyone survived a full life without getting old, or flu, or doubting their parents' beliefs?

Life in a traditional village, or a contemporary heteropolis, makes one hyper-conscious of a truth hidden by the usual binary logic. It is this: no matter how successful and well-positioned one may be in the dominant hierarchy, most of one's life will be spent on the margins, too old or too young to occupy the center for long – or simply too unlucky. The asymmetry of power, with one winner and countless losers, means that everybody for most of their lives is on the outside, on the periphery. At the same time, as the sheer number of differentiating relationships suggest, there are moments when one always has some power over others, power over one's own body and parts of the local environment. In other words, as Michel Foucault and others have argued, power is at once centralized and decentralized, part of a mainstream binary logic and sidestream multi-logic.

An important rediscovery of the 1960s was that self-created difference can be enjoyable and especially empowering if enjoyed.

The counter-culture, for a brief moment, established a coalition of convivial protesting groups – anti-War demonstrators, feminists, blacks, students and artists – who actually took pleasure in positioning themselves on the edge. Many individuals achieved personal identity by placing themselves against the center, thereby defining new sub-centers. Throughout the seventies this complex set of positions started to become progressively more articulated in North America, and triple structures appeared. The new logic became heterosexual male versus female and gay, white versus black and colored, rich versus poor and middle-class, youth culture versus the old and middle-aged – and countless other trialectic relationships emerged. While not progressive in every case, these articulations subverted the crushing binary logic of the establishment versus everybody else: pluralism was served.

In Los Angeles, as we have seen, a similar complexification has occurred, to the point where the periphery often is the center. More interesting things happen in city life on the outskirts than in Downtown; the 'ex-centrics' outperform their establishment counter-parts, the marginalized designers constantly assert their individuality against a conformist profession; and the sub-urbs and ex-urbs suddenly become more productive than the old urban centers. Oppositional logic is even stood on its head. With Frank Gehry's Disney Hall, for instance, we reach a cultural warp where *the* peripheralized architect and his ex-centric style have finally become embraced by the establishment right in its cultural heartland. Indeed, as is evident in the architectural magazines, en-formality is fast becoming a dominant style in more places than Los Angeles. Is this simply co-opting the opposition, token change or something deeper?

While the acceptance of one marginalized architect, and a style of difference, does not solve the general problem of marginalization, it does reveal the potency of developing a new mode of action on the periphery and ways in which a self-conscious otherness can be turned to advantage. Such creations as Disney Hall also contest the image of a central monoculture based on old symbols of dominance – classical columns, modern high-tech, overly ordered symmetries and centralized power structures – all the formulae of previous cultural centers in Los Angeles. The style of en-formality is important for defining public space or, rather, redefining it in such a way that different people can enter into a fluid social situation. Crossing of categories, fusing of boundaries, and ambiguous natural imagery allow marginalized groups to move more freely in space and identify momentarily with new images of otherness. Hetero-architecture condones pluralist behaviour, even if it does not promote, or represent, minoritization.

There are other ways Post-Modern Liberalism is moving beyond binary power-logic. As many minorities are discovering, social relations do not have to be defined from the periphery to the center, they can be made on the outside. Hence the rainbow coalition of marginalized groups – always, it is true, in danger of fission – hence Korean/black expressions of unity after the riots, hence the creation of Pan-Asian communities. Regarding the latter, Chinese, Japanese and Korean groups resent being lumped together by the public, and the federal census, under the label 'Asian' – as much as different cultures of blacks and whites are offended by the same treatment – but, like other groups, they are willing to adopt a category of self-classification, and a form of organization, if it is voluntary.

With the 'browning of America', that is the shift to a predominantly colored labor force that is on the horizon, we will probably see a host of alliances on the periphery, and they will probably gain in power. The 'Asian-Pacific American' and 'Latino-American' might contest the 'Anglo-Atlantic American' as the sole dominant identity. If such a shift takes place and a pluralistic-dominant emerges, then the liberal goal of respecting difference would be considerably deepened. As it is, the concept of 'Anglo' is now hybrid and diffuse enough to be a polite synonym for anyone who is a non-Hispanic white. Furthermore, because of commercialization, the dominant no longer has any clear *cultural* definition. This flattening and coarsening of WASP identity is not, of course, a deepening of cultural values, but it does allow other voices and identities to merge with the dominant, and is positive in that sense. Besides, when WASP identity becomes publicly mixed up with George Bush and John Major, and the two Anglo countries become two of the leading debtors, the value of the label is liable to get muddier still. The direction is obvious, but still missed by commentators: a world meta-culture is now diffusing the nature of the dominant and its representation.

Global shifts in demography and economics are likely to be mirrored in political power and culture as the center-periphery model breaks up into a constellation or network. The East-West binary pair has ended with the freeze-out of the Cold War, to be replaced by what is variously called the Single Superpower, the Pax Americana, or the

New World Disorder. In reality, with the Group of Seven, the UN and coalition-building, the emergent structure may be more like the inefficient network of the L.A. County Department of Animal Control than either a megapower or chaos; it works, but only somewhat.

Probably the United States, itself a nation-state of nations, will evolve towards a weak, decentralized macro-system, a situation that would again increase the power of minorities, the fifty States and other groupings. Pluralism again would be deepened. In any case, one thing is clear from the multicultural debate: there is no single privileged axis of difference – race, class and gender always contesting for the top position as most crucial – but, rather, eight or so key dimensions of identity-formation. Since the debate, and dialogic, have now made such truths clear, it means that whatever the future holds it will be a complex mixture of many dimensions, with many solutions, not a privileged few. The heteropolis may become a hyperspace – a multi-dimensional field, in the language of physics – of identity and power-relations.

The missing element in this emergent pluralism is an emphasis on what people have in common, what values and mutual destiny they share. From a negative viewpoint, however, it is not particularly hard to see what common fate is fast approaching. Any conference on environmental pollution and species extinction, that is not run by modernists, reveals the grim reality: some twenty-seven thousand species of plants and animals are going under every year – seventy-four a day, three an hour – which gives us about fifty years before we, as all other creatures, join hands – or D.N.A. or whatever – in the final communion.[66] What the multicultural debate has somehow over-looked, in its preoccupation with human rights, is that, while proclaiming democracy, we have snuffed out the lives of more and more creatures, or as Thomas Berry puts it:

> If democracy is so wonderful, why is a democratic country [the United States] doing so much damage. I describe democracy as 'a conspiracy of humans against the natural world'. And the North American Constitution as 'the conspiracy of the Citizens of this country against the continent'. So what I'm asking for is a *real* Constitution for the North American continent that would include the 'tree nation' and the 'bird nation' and all the different components of the community. *That*

would be a real and acceptable democracy. American Indians always thought in these terms and they used those words – 'bird nation' and 'tree nation'.[67]

There is no question that we will be forced by ecological pressures to acknowledge our common dependence on the larger Earth community from which we spring and on which we depend. The present political denial of this, reinforced by modernist ideology, will not be possible in twenty years. Not only will films like *Blade Runner* dramatize the message of the L.A. eco-collapse, but also pollution-counts, like those in Mexico City, which will keep everybody reaching for their respirators.

Such negative predictions are easy to make and not enough to change one's mind, or heart, entirely – which is one reason the environmental movement has largely shifted its emphasis from warning towards persuasion, from the negative consequences which come from denial to the positive aspects which can come from enjoying our connection to the living world. Quite naturally individuals do not feel responsible for the environmental crisis. It was created absent-mindedly by their consuming too much, or by their ancestors, or by the Fortune 500 companies and big industry. Since it was not caused by conscious decision, most people feel surprised when the guilt is laid squarely at their garage-door. In L.A., however, the place where the name and fact of smog was invented in the 1940s, the denial is coming to an end. In what has been called the largest spending-program except for defense, $185 billion will be devoted to combating the fumes, again not with one but a variety of solutions, from electric cars to public transport to tele-commuting.

For ecologists, bioregionalists, Friends of the Earth, Gaians and other marginalized protestors, forging a convivial identity on the Green fringe, such partial solutions, however desirable, will never be enough. The problems of a modern technocratic civilization will always keep one step ahead of any ameliorations because the reigning ideology of continual human growth – both numerical and economic – is unrealistic. It will continue to manufacture new problems, equivalents of the greenhouse effect and the hole in the ozone layer. No matter how many piecemeal solutions to these are instituted, the problems will go on multiplying because, for the first time in history, humanity rather than the Earth has become the dominant background. The players have become the stage.

In the past forty years the population has doubled to more than five billion while the fossil fuel consumption has quadrupled. Economists, modernists and politicians like to foreground the attendant quadrupling of the gross world product and conveniently overlook the likelihood that the oxymoron 'uneconomic growth' is next: further increases in GNP may actually impoverish the whole global biosphere. Although there is as yet no accounting system to measure real wealth, many claim we have already reached this paradoxical point.[68]

Such disturbing thoughts turn the mind back on itself towards an area where individuals can make a difference – to a specific city and place. Here the philosophy of bioregionalism is relevant, a movement which started in the 1970s that now has some sixty groups working in North America. These ecologists focus attention on one's specific region, with its existing life-forms, before human concerns and reversing the anthropomorphism of the reigning paradigms. The motivating idea is to understand and appreciate the particularities and requirements of a place and reassert its primacy as the background for human activity. Kirkpatrick Sale puts the agenda of bioregionalists:

> . . . to become dwellers in the land, to relearn the laws of Gaia, to come to know the earth fully and honestly, the crucial and perhaps only and all-encompassing task is to understand *place*, the immediate specific place where we live. The kinds of soils and rocks under our feet; the source of the waters we drink; the meaning of the different kinds of winds; the common insects, birds, mammals, plants, and trees; the particular cycles of the seasons; the times to plant and harvest and forage – these are the things necessary to know. The limits of its resources; the carrying capacities of its lands and waters; the places where it must not be stressed; the places where its bounties can best be developed; the treasures it holds and the treasures it withholds – these are the things which must be understood. And the cultures of the people, of the populations native to the land and of those who have grown up with it, the human social and economic arrangements shaped by and adapted to the geomorphic ones, in both urban and rural settings – these are the things that must be appreciated. That, in essence, is bioregionalism.[69]

Broadly stated these must also become the goals of heteropolitans as they come to understand the possibilities of the new city form. Understand and appreciate the existing *place* – in the case of Los Angeles not only the bountiful provision of three hundred and twenty days of sun and a temperate climate, of mountains, open space and ocean, but now also the incredible variety of people and animals, the second and third growths of flora and fauna that make it such an interesting and satisfying place to be.

In the introduction I mentioned my surprise at discovering the New Eden of Beasts that has wandered into the region along with the waves of settlers and immigrants, the hidden animal kingdom. This has remained veiled even to those, such as my teacher Reyner Banham, who can write books about L.A. with a subtitle featuring 'the four ecologies'. Ecology without animals? It seems like one of the more egregious oversights. But not myself knowing much about the subject, I questioned several biology professors on the city's animal distribution: 'Is there a map of animal diversity, does anyone know what animals inhabit L.A. and where?' The experts are agnostic on such questions; and if they are, what is the prospect for bioregionalists trying to understand and appreciate the particularities of the place?

It struck me after I had written this book that I too had missed the point of heteromorphia which was under my nose, for one of the most striking aspects of increasing pluralization in Los Angels existed right outside my windows in Rustic Canyon: the variety of plants brought into the city that have continued to flourish. Rustic Canyon, called 'the closest jungle to Downtown', has the most extraordinary collection of Eucalyptus trees in North America. These were planted at the turn of the century by Abbott Kinney, the man who created 'Venice L.A.' with its equally foreign canals, Romanesque arcades and Italian details. He wanted to discover what would grow well and fast: nearly everthing did, including seventy-two species of Eucalyptus, acacia and pine trees, many over a hundred feet tall. While this canyon is especially varied because of his planting program, the other canyons and foothills also have an increasingly diverse flora, as indeed does the L.A. basin as a whole. For the most part this increase in species richness is allowed by the diversion of water from the Colorado River and, in that sense, it is hardly a result of the bioregion. Human interference has turned the city into an amazing garden, a growing zoo for global exotica where, according to the Kinney-inspired adage 'everything grows, given enough water'. Since then there have been several years of low rainfall (until recently) and water is potentially more scarce due to population growth. Many L.A. gardeners and landscape architects – unwilling to give up the idea of the city as exotic garden – are now planting drought-resistant species. They are returning to desert plants, to native specimens, but with a sensibility altered by recent ecological history and the view that Los Angeles can be a 'world-garden', the growing equivalent of a world city.

The long-term sustainability of this policy is, of course, in question, but the great variety of flora is a present fact. It awaits a botanist, zoologist or ecologist to catalogue and sing its pleasures, to tell us about the importance of this place as we find it. As the heteropolitan-bioregionalist says, 'See the world and love it; stay at home'.

*Los Angeles' varied flora, collated and drawn by Maggie Keswick illustrating the adage that 'anything can grow in L.A. given enough water'. The mild climate, good top-soil and water diverted from the Colorado River have given the city a greater diversity of plant life than any comparable urban area in the world and, like the inhabitants, most of the plants are immigrants. Among the sixty most planted species shown here only six are California natives. The variety of foreign origins is extraordinary, a diversity that has remained largely unknown: even today no accurate census of the plant population exists.*

*The native flora, adapted to long dry summers, was first removed to make way for irrigated agriculture (including citrus). Then, as urbanization spread, this in turn was replaced by quick-growing trouble-free street shade trees which landscapers preferred to what they considered the 'temperamental' local plants. A startling study made during the five-year drought of the eighties showed that, on average, half a family home's water went on lawns – and that they were getting twice the water they needed! Fashions in planting change: today's industrial sites are less likely to be planted with the Brazilian Pepper (Schinus terebinthus) than the Mexican Shamel Ash (Fraxinus uhdei). Old commercial sites were often shaded by the Chinese camphor (Cinnamomum camphora); new developments prefer carrotwood (Cupaniopsis anacardioides) and Kaffir plum (Harpephyllum caffrum).*

*The beautiful native California sycamores (Plantanus racemosa) and evergreen live oaks (Quercus agrifolia) remain important L.A. trees, and the resurgence of interest in drought-resistant plants is likely to add to, rather than reduce, the great diversity of flora.*

*(Based on information supplied by Nancy Goslee Power Associates and the Valley Research Corporation, Van Nuys.)*

## FOOTNOTES

1 *Multiculturalism and 'The Politics of Recognition' – An Essay by Charles Taylor With Commentary by Amy Gutman*, edited by Steven C. Rockefeller, Michael Walzer and Susan Wolf, Princeton University Press, Princeton, New Jersey, 1992.

2 Walter Truett Anderson, *Reality Isn't What it Used to Be, Theatrical Politics, Ready-to-Wear Religion, Global Myths, Primitive Chic and the Wonders of the Post-Modern World*, Harper & Row, San Francisco 1990.

3 Hazel Rose Markus, the social psychologist at the University of Michigan, has discussed 'possible selves'; Kenneth Gergen, author of *The Saturated Self: Dilemmas of Identity in Contemporary Life*, also treats the question of multiple selves and the way they are socially constructed.

4 Rem Koolhaas, *Delirious New York*, Oxford University Press, New York, 1978, p13. For Koolhaas each of the 2028 New York City blocks democratically fosters a different style, group, interest or 'mania'.

5 Such observations became, in the 1980s, the repeated wisdom of articles on Los Angeles; see for instance Charles Lockwood and Christopher B. Leinberger, 'Los Angeles Comes of Age', *The Atlantic Monthly*, January 1988, p91.

6 Claritas is a research corporation that specializes in marketing information. They have kindly provided us with information for the maps and a description of 'lifestyle clusters' – a creation of their's which they use as a marketing tool. A general review of the field can be found in Michael J. Weiss, *The Clustering of America*, Harper Row, New York, 1988.

7 For this information see Richard S. Wurman, *L.A./ACCESS*, Access Press, Los Angeles, 1981, p113.

8 Popular and architectural critics both see the undistinguished nature of Downtown skyscrapers. For a recent view see Mike Davis, 'Chinatown Revisited?', *Sex, Death and God in L.A.*, edited by David Reid, Pantheon, 1992, p27; and for an older one, Reyner Banham, *Los Angeles, The Architecture of the Four Ecologies*, Penguin Books, Harmondsworth, 1971, pp208-11.

9 The original *L.A. School* was initiated by George Rand and myself, had its first meeting at the Biltmore Hotel under the auspices of Gene Summers, and included, if memory is correct, Roland Coate, Peter De Bretteville, Frank Gehry, Craig Hodgetts, Coy Howard, Eugene Kupper, Tony Lumsden, Thom Mayne, Robert Mangurian, Charles Moore, Cesar Pelli, Stephanos Polyzoides, Michael Rotondi, Tim Vreeland and Buzz Yudell. The L.A. Museum of Architecture project started in 1989, was initiated by Nancy Pinckert and myself, and includes a much wider group of Los Angeles architects. There have also been other loose groupings, including that of Aaron Betsky's and Christian Hubert's *L.A. Forum for Architecture and Urban Design*, mostly for younger, more radical architects. The L.A. School of geographers and planners had a quite separate and independent formulation in the 1980s, which stemmed from the analysis of the city as a new post-modern urban type. Allen Scott, Ed Soja, Michael Storper, Michael Dear and Mike Davis are among its protagonists. Its themes vary from L.A. as the post-Fordist, post-modern city of contradictions, to the Exopolis of many fragments in search of a unity, to the nightmare city of social inequities.

10 *Experimental Architecture in Los Angeles*, Introduction by Frank Gehry, Essays by Aaron Betsky, John Chase and Leon Whiteson, Los Angeles Forum for Architecture and Urban Design, Rizzoli, New York, 1991. The back cover and pp47-48, 88, refer to the Gehry-Schule etc, while Gehry denies it three times, p10.

11 Conversation with Frank Gehry, April 1992. It is true, there are important differences between Gehry and his followers. Nevertheless, still present are common attitudes towards material, 'en-formality', adhocism, hybridization and, above all, heterogeneity.

12 Leon Whiteson, 'Young Architects in Los Angeles, Social, Political and Cultural Context', *Experimental Architecture in Los Angeles*, op cit note 10, pp84-89, quote p88.

13 The Newsom brothers, in their promotional brochures, made these claims; see Joseph C. Newsom, *Picturesque and Artistic Homes and Buildings of California*, San Francisco, 1890. This work was finally brought to public attention by the historians David Gebhard and Robert Winter.

14 Thom Mayne has not made this point, and is not acquainted with the Newsom's work, but, judging from his remarks on other architects, like Gehry, Moss and others in the L.A. School, he would find their work too cloying.

15 Charles Moore, quoted in Robert Stern, *New Directions in American Architecture*, George Braziller, New York, 1969, p70.

16  See Charles Moore, 'Working Together to Make Something', *Architectural Record*, Felmay, 1984, pp102-103.

17  Frank Gehry, *Experimental Architecture in Los Angeles*, *op cit*, note 10, p9.

18  The Museum saga is a long and complex one. Suffice it to say that, first, the 'competition' was 'won' by a Canadian developer – 'bought' would be a better term – over the superior urban scheme of Robert McGuire's team. Then Isozaki's Museum project, the best part of the Canadian scheme, was disputed by a group of artists and an architect, Coy Howard, who wanted a background design. After much dramatic maneuvering using the press, Isozaki was able to regain design control and produce the building; a donor, Max Pavlevsky, then withdrew his gift.

19  Charles Moore, 'You Have to Pay For the Public Life', *Perspecta 9/10*, New Haven, 1965, pp57-97.

20  Amy Wallace, 'Like It's So L.A.! Not Really', *Los Angeles Times*, February 29, 1992, pA1, A22, A23.

21  *Ibid*, A23.

22  Aaron Betsky, *Violated Perfection*, Chapter 8 'Technomorphism', Rizzoli, New York, 1990, pp183-203.

23  Kisho Kurokawa, *Rediscovering Japanese Space*, Weatherhill, New York and Tokyo, 1988, pp70-77; Intercultural Architecture, Academy Editions, London 1992, pp19-27.

24  Thom Mayne, lecture at UCLA, April 1992 and unpublished manuscript, April 6, 1992, p8.

25  *Ibid*.

26  See *op cit*, note 2, p36.

27  For an analysis of Frank Israel's Bright and Associates see Sylvia Lavin, 'Creativity Begets Creativity', *Designers' West*, September 1990, pp68-75.

28  *Eric Owen Moss, Buildings and Projects*, Preface Philip Johnson, Introduction Wolf Prix, Rizzoli, New York, 1991, p14.

29  *Ibid*, p15.

30  *Ibid*, p13.

31  *Ibid*, pp12, 15.

32  For Mikhail Bakhtin's notions of dialogic and heteroglossia see Michael Holquist, *Dialogism, Bakhtin and his World*, Routledge, London and New York, 1990; Tzvetan Todorov, *Mikhail Bakhtin, The Dialogical Principle*, Manchester University Press, 1986.

33  For a very good analysis of the rioters' motives, several of the quotes, and maps of the spreading violence, refer to Ashley Dunn and Shawn Hubler, 'Unlikely Flash Point for Riots', *L.A. Times,* July 5, 1992, A1, pp18-20. Tulasi Srivinas very kindly supplied this and other articles on the riots.

34  For an excellent understanding of the riots refer to Mike Davis, 'In L.A., Burning All Illusions', *The Nation*, June 1, 1992, pp743-46; quote p743. Charlene Spretnak very kindly sent this and other articles.

35  Troy Duster, *L.A. Times*, July 5, 1992, p20.

36  Paul Lieberman, 'More Hispanics Charged than Blacks in Unrest', *International Herald Tribune*, June 19, 1992.

37  Civil Disaster Damage Survey, Department of Building and Safety, Los Angeles, File Run as of 8/3/92. The first five most damaged building types were: retail store sixty-eight per cent; restaurants six per cent; gas stations five per cent; offices five per cent; single family dwellings three per cent; apartments three per cent. The other building types comprised two and one per cent.

38  Paul Ong and Evelyn Blumenberg, 'Income and Racial Inequality in Los Angeles', draft October 1992, p23, soon to appear in *Los Angeles – California*, edited by Allen Scott, University of California Press, 1993.

39  Davis, *op cit,* note 34, p744.

40  Ong and Blumenberg, *op cit*, note 38, p25.

41  Barbara Vobejda, 'An L.A. Snapshot: Racial Change and Economic Strains', *International Herald Tribune*, date lost (June 1992?).

42  Ched Myers, 'Looking for Justice, Holding the Peace', *Sojourners*, November, 1992, pp30-33.

43  Robert Reinhold, 'Six Months After Riots, Los Angeles Still Bleeds', *New York Times*, November 1, 1992, p14.

44  *Ibid*.

45  Davis, *op cit*, note 34.

46 'L.A. Greens offer enterprise zone alternative', *Green Consensus*, November 1992, p1.

47 Anthony Vidler, *The Architectural Uncanny, Essays in the Modern Unhomely*, MIT Press, Cambridge, 1992.

48 Mike Davis, 'Frank Gehry as Dirty Harry' in *City of Quartz, Excavating the Future in Los Angeles*, Verso, London/New York, 1990, pp236-240.

49 For a discussion of post-riot L.A. defensible architecture and this point, see 'A City Behind Walls', *Newsweek*, October 5, 1992, pp68-69.

50 Mrs Disney has pledged $50 million; a major public parking lot and the rest of the building will be paid for by the city. Journalists, critics and politicians raised the question of whether the Disney Hall would be culturally unifying even before the riots – see Whiteson's defense of the building, below. After the riots such questions became more prevalent, as I found when a BBC director, making a *Late Show* film on Gehry, put them to me and other people who know Gehry's work.

51 Leon Whiteson, 'High Note, Gehry's Crown for Bunker Hill is a Fitting Tribute for Disney', *Los Angeles Times*, Sunday, September 15, 1991, Real Estate Section, K1, 14, 15.

52 *ibid*.

53 *ibid*.

54 'Disney Hall "Work of Art" or Wet Cardboard', Letters, *Los Angeles Times*, September 29, 1991.

55 Gordon Dillow, 'Stop the Disney Concert Hall', *Downtown News*, Los Angeles, September 18, 1991, p14.

56 Linda Hutcheon, *A Poetics of Postmodernism, History, Theory, Fiction*, Routledge, New York/London, 1988; my own writings on post-modern architecture since 1975 defined this fundamental agenda of double-coding.

57 Quoted from Steven C Rockefeller, 'Comment', in *Multiculturism and the 'Politics of Recognition', An Essay by Charles Taylor with a Commentary by Amy Gutman*, *op cit*, note 1, pp93-4.

58 *Ibid*, p38.

59 Mead quoted by Taylor, *op cit*, p32.

60 Stephanie Chavez, 'Hard Times at Fairfax High', *Los Angeles Times*, January 29, 1993, ppB1, B2.

61 Sir Isiah Berlin, 'Nationalism: The Melting Pot Myth', Bryan Magee in Conversation with Sir Isiah Berlin, Sir Brian Urquhart and Professor Geofrey Hosking, produced by Matt Thompson, BBC, Radio 3, February 19, 1992.

62 The figure of forty-eight is taken from an article and chart in David Binder and Barbara Crossette, 'As Ethnic Wars Multiply, U.S. Strives for a Policy', *New York Times*, February 7, 1993, pp1,12.

63 Henry Kamm, 'Migrants Wear Out Welcome As Numbers Grow in Europe', *New York Times*, February 10, 1993, pp1, 6.

64 'The Other Fortress Europe', *The Economist*, June 1, 1991, p45; see also Joel Kokkin, *Tribes, How Race, Religion and Identity Determine Success in the New Global Economy*, Random House, New York, 1993, p259.

65 *ibid*, p6.

66 Species extinction is an inexact science which has increased in accuracy especially since Berkeley scientists Walter and Luis Alvarez's researches in the late 1970s. For some up-to-date views see David M. Raup, *Extinction, Bad Genes or Bad Luck?* W.W. Norton & Co, New York and London, 1991; Edward O. Wilson, *The Diversity of Life*, Harvard University, Cambridge, Massachusetts, 1992; and for a good popular presentation, Rick Gore, 'The March Toward Extinction', *National Geographic*, June 1989, pp662-99. The figures for yearly species extinction vary from thirty to ten thousand, but all agree that humanity is now the main cause of mass slaughter, a decimation that has not occurred since the last natural disaster sixty-five million years ago.

67 'Conversation with Thomas Berry', *Our Way Into the Future*, Global Perspectives, Box 925, Sonoma, California, 95476, Tape 2, 1992.

68 'Uneconomic growth', an oxymoron for economists, has been around as a concept at least since the Club of Rome's report in 1972. For a very good analysis see Herman E Daly and John B. Cobb Jr, *For the Common Good, Redirecting the Economy Toward Community, the Environment and a Sustainable Future*, Beacon Press, Boston, 1989.

69 Kirkpatrick Sale, *Dwellers in the Land: The Bioregional Vision*, Sierra Club Books, San Francisco, 1985, p42.

# CO-OPERATE L.A.

*The Green Party of California, Los Angeles County Proposal for Reconstruction and Rebuilding in Los Angeles, written by Dennis Bottum, Mike Feinstein and Watt Sheasby*

The events following the acquittal of the LAPD officers who beat Rodney King have exposed the reality of life in Los Angeles. The burning, the violence and the utter breakdown of social order stem from long standing social, economic and political injustices. It is not surprising that citizens who have no stake in their society, who feel they have little or no control over their lives and communities, have struck back against the structures of society. Contrary to its depiction by much of the media, this 'revolt' cut across racial lines. Similar negative social conditions are endemic in many communities: economic and political powerlessness accompanied by homelessness, despair and anger. The problems are deep and structural and any plans to 'rebuild L.A.' must address change at this level.

For far too long the Los Angeles economy has served 'outside' capital at the expense of local communities and the environment. The Ueberroth 'Rebuild L.A.' Commission believes that it can continue this practice. It hasn't worked before and it won't work now. 'Rebuild L.A.' must be replaced with a broad community-wide coalition to 'Co-operate L.A.'

Only policies that promote community self-determination and self-reliance can lead us to a just and sustainable society. Enterprise zones and trickle-down economics are more of the same old failed policies. They disempower communities and drive down wages, working conditions and the quality of the environment. Therefore, the Green Party proposes that all reconstruction and future development incorporate the following key principles:

## SELF DETERMINATION

Local and community control over economic and political decisions affecting the community. Where decisions affect more than one community, communities need to confederate on regional, state and national levels.

## SUSTAINABILITY

Conservation and improvement of a community's resource base (its natural wealth of people, animals, land and environmental systems) to improve the quality of life for this and future generations.

## COMMUNITY-BASED CO-OPERATIVE ECONOMICS

New economic structures and institutions should support local ownership and control; should broaden the industrial and commercial base to provide for greater community self-reliance; and should recycle profits back into the community. These economic structures should promote co-operative, community-based forms of entrepreneurship which sustain and strengthen the community.

To integrate these principles into rebuilding L.A., the Green Party recommends the following:

## COMMUNITY BANK SYSTEM

The creation of a community-based system of banks would establish access to capital for local and regional business development. Start-up funding would come from a mix of government and private sources. Some government funding could come from a state tax on various luxury items. Some private funding could come from private financial institutions. Lending and distribution of funds would conform to community guide-lines and be accountable to review by a community-based board of trustees. The geographic lending activity of all commercial financial institutions should be publicly disclosed and ranked. These banks would promote the welfare of the communities they serve by promoting local production to meet local needs, by co-operatively owned and managed businesses and ecologically sound forms of production and business that hire from within the communities where they are located.

### COMMUNITY CO-OPERATIVE ENTERPRISE SUPPORT PROGRAMS

Rather than creating 'enterprise zones' that promote investment and control from outside the community, 'co-operative zones' would insure that profits are recycled within the community to create jobs and prosperity. Co-operative zone funding would help train people to develop and manage their local businesses and provide assistance, such as 'business incubators', to help new businesses through the early stages of development. Joint ventures would be encouraged between local businesses and the larger business community, but only when these ventures would assist in the capitalization or increased expertise of the local firms while leaving them in control of their own destiny.

Beyond the selective rebuilding of locally owned small businesses, funding would also focus on creating neighborhood owned, co-operative and democratically managed businesses, including: co-operative food markets, health care facilities, savings and credit institutions, laundromats, day-care centers, recycling plants, manufacturing plants utilizing locally-recycled materials, shopping and recreational centers or other businesses as the community may decide.

### A COMMUNITY DEVELOPMENT CORPORATION

Accountable to community-based boards of trustees, the Community Development Corporation would acquire and develop property within the community to assist the development of community-based, co-operative and ecological enterprises. Planning for development would begin with an inventory of community businesses and services. It would employ a planning process responsive to community needs and provide ample opportunity for public involvement, including a public meeting process conforming to the Brown Act. It would promote ecological, human-scale development, such as ecological building and landscaping, pedestrian-oriented planning, urban forests and parks, community gardens and public transportation that truly serves the community.

### THE U.S. MAYORS CONFERENCE DOMESTIC MARSHAL PLAN: A SHIFT IN PUBLIC SPENDING

There should be promotion of Local Exchange Trading Systems within neighborhoods and between neighborhoods. LETSystems promote direct and third party barter and barter/cash exchange of services, goods, tools and food between individuals within a community. LETSystems promote local self-reliance by circulating goods and services within a community, by lessening the exit of a community's wealth and purchasing power, and by making a community less dependant upon outside economic and trade policies.

### AFFORDABLE HOUSING

We support people's right to control their own housing, whether that housing be individually or co-operatively owned and managed. However, we feel that by itself, the Department of Housing and Urban Development's (HUD) plan to privatize public housing units is the wrong approach to dealing with the housing crisis. HUD's plan is not only an attempt on the part of the government to abandon its responsibility to provide publicly financed housing; but by privatizing public housing without also affecting the underlying economic conditions that influence housing costs and availability, the HUD plan will only accelerate current economic patterns which have helped produce the housing crisis in the first place. Immediate steps should be taken to refurbish existing public housing and to enforce building codes at the direction of elected tenant governing boards. Unused properties should be identified and utilized for emergency housing of the homeless.

On a more structural level we favor, as has been done in Pittsburgh, a gradual shift in the proportion of the property tax base from buildings towards land. Our current property tax structure encourages holding prime sites idle, using them for parking lots or letting housing units fall into disrepair, by levying higher taxes on buildings and any 'improvements' such as renovation and maintenance of housing. A shift in the property tax from buildings to land will bring land prices down by taking the speculative advantage out of holding land. Lower land prices, together with lower taxes on buildings, would in turn bring about lower housing costs and the building of more housing units. Overall, a shift in the property tax from buildings to land would rejuvenate and promote efficient land use in urban centers.

Complimenting the property tax shift, we favor a major long-term program, implemented at the regional level, of constructing co-operative housing which would be owned by tenants in community land trusts. A land-trust program would create and preserve affordable housing. We also favor identifying existing properties that could be taken out of the commodity market and put into community land trusts. As part of achieving this, we favor purchasing housing units that are in need of improvement and putting them into trust at a low cost before improvements are made. Construction for all housing should use low-cost, ecological, state-of-the-art materials and techniques. Construction should utilize local labor and expertise as much as possible.

### COMMUNITY-POLICE RELATIONS

Proposition 'F' attempts to address some of the problems of the Los Angeles Police Department with reforms and a term limit. In as far as this limited effort goes, we supported it. But other changes are also necessary. The police will continue to be seen as an 'occupying force' until they are fully accountable to the people they are supposed to serve and protect. Specific programs should be established to recruit community members into the LAPD to serve in their own communities. Police officers need to 'belong' to the community they serve. All police officers also should be trained in non-violent resolution techniques.

A full-time, community-based Civilian Police Review Board, elected and salaried, should be established, with the power to prosecute police abuse. Also community-based conflict management teams could be established, perhaps under the direction of community councils (see below).

### EDUCATING VS INCARCERATING

The Bush Administration's Operation 'Weed and Seed', with its emphasis on criminalization and imprisonment of young men, will only escalate inner-city conflict and further devastate lives and communities. Instead of putting more millions into incarceration, the money should be spent on education and job training. The highest quality education should be available where the worst deprivations and disadvantages exist.

### COMMUNITY COUNCILS, COMMUNICATION

We strongly urge the formation of community councils throughout Los Angeles to discuss and oversee community issues. Informed communities are the basis of a strong and truly democratic society. Every community should have a communications network assisted by small-scale radio stations and computer networks which could provide a greater sharing of ideas and encourage broader community participation.

### POLITICAL REFORM

The size of the Los Angeles City Council should be increased to reflect neighborhood constituencies of fifty to seventy-five thousand people. The size of the Los Angeles County Board of Supervisors should be increased to reflect constituencies of one hundred to two hundred people. To organize for the 'Co-operate L.A.' agenda, a broad, multi-racial coalition should be built now to unite all those interested individuals and groups seeking to find true and lasting solutions. Unless these forces unite, the lessons of the L.A. uprising will be lost in a petty and divisive competition for the crumbs dispensed from above.

### LAND USE: ECOLOGICAL, HUMAN-SCALE DESIGN

Our aims are the following, to:

• promote increase of open space, including urban forests, parks and community gardens

• combine trees and other greenery for a cooling effect in urban design, and increase planting of trees overall

• promote pedestrian-oriented, human scale urban design

• increase bike usability

• promote mixed use planning to decrease commuting and to build community

• promote timely, convenient and affordable public transportation

• provide for a community process to plan transportation routes that do not disrupt traditional neighborhoods

• promote efficient water use and water recycling and encourage drought resistant landscaping

• promote urban agriculture and organic gardening through community gardens, market gardens and roof gardens

• provide space for neighborhood and inter-neighborhood barter of food, tools, services and goods and for farmers' markets

• promote community recycling, including community manufacturing utilizing recycled materials

• strictly prohibit the production and dumping of toxic wastes in production processes within the community

• promote energy-efficiency and conservation in new construction and in the retrofitting of existing structures

• promote passive and active solar design to lessen community dependence upon energy utilities and corporations

• promote construction utilizing non-toxic and recycled materials

# INDEX